I Was Slept On

Mission:    To Proclaim Transformation and Truth
Publisher: Transformed Publishing, Cocoa, FL
Website:    www.transformedpublishing.com
Email:      transformedpublishing@gmail.com

This work is based on the author's life experiences, lifestyle, personal opinion, and recollection of events. It is a memoir, written with discretion, and without slanderous intention. To share his story, the author was granted permission to mention the names of people who were a part of his journey. Other names were fictitiously changed.

Any resemblance to someone else's life experiences, actual events or locales or persons, living or dead, is entirely coincidental.

ISBN: 978-1-953241-66-5 (paperback)
ISBN: 978-1-953241-67-2 (hardcover)
ISBN: 978-1-953241-68-9 (Ebook)

# I WAS SLEPT ON

Trashon "Tray Plus" Waller

# Acknowledgements

To begin with, I thank God for giving me life and the ability to write this book.

Secondly, I thank my parents for bringing me into this world. As a kid, my mother told me I could be anything I wanted to become if I put my mind to it. That stuck with me throughout my life, and I never doubted myself.

Even though my biological father wasn't around much, I appreciate him. Without him, there wouldn't be me.

I thank my grandmothers, Joan and Di, for always showing me unconditional love and giving me so much wisdom.

My late grandfather, Andrew Hall, I miss him so much and would like to thank him for displaying his natural strength throughout the roughest times.

I thank my big sister, Karesha, for always being a listening ear and giving me good advice even if it was something I didn't want to hear.

I acknowledge my daughters, Azaria and Taliyah. My girls are my world and they motivated me to change my life for the better.

I thank the mother of my child, Octavia, for coming into my life and being a part of my transformation. When I finished writing each chapter, I read it out loud to her. She motivated me to finish this book and chase my dreams.

I thank all my supporters for believing in me and supporting everything I do.

I also appreciate the people who doubted me and told me I wasn't good enough. They made me work ten times harder, not to prove them wrong but to prove me right about myself.

I give a special thanks to Mrs. Diana Robinson, with Transformed Publishing, for believing in my book and helping me become a published author.

Last but not least, I acknowledge myself. I'm thankful I didn't believe the doubt. I'm thankful I never gave up on myself when things were difficult. It took a lot to reflect on my entire life and put it all in a book. I'm thankful to be alive and chasing my dreams.

I couldn't have done it without God.

-Thank You

# TABLE OF CONTENTS

# 1

# Project Baby

My mother, my everything, Yolanda Hall, was twenty years old providing for her two-year-old daughter while pregnant with me, Trashon "Tray Plus" Waller. My mother was young, pretty, smart, and to top it all off, she was really from the hood.

My mom met my dad early in life as kids, then they became good friends. My dad had NFL dreams. I was told he was a handsome, muscular, spoiled young man. I guess he figured he could have any woman he wanted. After getting my mom pregnant with my sister at the age of sixteen he moved on to baby number two from another woman. Then two more women after that.

Somehow, in the middle of it all, the love my parents had for one another never died. My dad and my mother ended up rekindling their flame. Spring of 1990, March 24th, at Wuesthoff hospital a star was born. I was my mom's second and final child. I was my dad's third oldest out of five.

My mom knew I was special since day one. My dad wanted me to take after him and become a junior. My mom wasn't going for it, so they came to an agreement and named me Trashon.

My dad wasn't around much. I don't know the full story. I can only remember my stepfather Rick bringing me home from the hospital at the age of four after being diagnosed with chickenpox. My stepfather was the only father I knew. He was there for me since I was a baby. He took care of the whole household, and he told my mother she didn't have to work at all.

Growing up in Cocoa, Florida in the projects in the early 90's was a time to be alive. I didn't come from a wealthy family. My mother's mother and father had a drug addiction. They were a part of the big 80s crack cocaine epidemic. My grandparents never exposed us to their bad habits. In my eyes my grandparents were the best grandparents ever. The things they instilled in me as a child, money cannot buy.

1995

By the age of five, I was *outside.* I was hanging with my uncle A. My uncle A lived with us. He was my mother's youngest sibling and more like a big brother I never had. We are exactly ten years apart. Just by me being *outside* with him at an early age gave me a head start.

By the time I could read, I was already listening to my Walkman and rapping 2Pac lyrics. My uncle used to have me listen to all the hot rap artists of that time. I have always had a love for music. Growing up, I recorded all my favorite songs from the radio onto my cassette tapes and learned the lyrics the same day.

By me being such a cool little dude and so advanced, I gained some older Godbrothers in my hood. My uncle A's friends became my big brothers - John, Jermaine, and J. Everybody knew not to play with them because they meant business. I learned how to get money, how to protect myself, and how to be a stand-up guy, just by hanging around all of them at a young age.

Their mother, Mrs. Margaret, is the best Godmother a kid could ask for. Every time I brought home good grades, she used to reward me and buy me Jordans or whatever I wanted. I love her so much. Like I said, it was a time to be alive. There was so much love in the air.

We really went outside and actually played. I met a lot of friends growing up in the projects, some became brothers. My peers always had the utmost respect for me. I was always the cool fun friend who everyone wanted to be around, and I didn't mind getting into trouble.

My Auntie Tania's kids were my best friends growing up. My cousins KiKi, Si, and I were a tight click. They are my girl cousins, but they do not play about Tray.

Our parents let us play until the streetlight came on. If that streetlight came on and you weren't in the house, it was an automatic whipping. I received some of the worst whippings from my mom. There isn't anything worse than getting caught fresh out of the tub and still wet. *Ouch!* I get it, I was a very hardheaded child. Sometimes I think to myself, *Did I really deserve all that? Was I really that bad?* (Laughing my butt off.)

I have always been super smart, curious, and too advanced for my age. Now, I appreciate all those whippings. They made me who I am today and taught me a lot about self-respect.

# 2
# How It Was Growing Up

Growing up in the projects was cool. A lot of my cousins and friends stayed in the same neighborhood. I witnessed some fun times and some hard times at a young age.

Plenty of nights my sister and I had to bathe in the same water to save money by not running up the water bill. I remember times we boiled water to take a bath because the hot water was not working. We had our moments of struggle just like everybody I knew in our neighborhood. Some of my friends had it worse than we did so I never complained and considered my situation a blessing. We went through our rough times together. As a whole, my mother and stepfather did the best they could for us, and I sincerely thank them for that.

My biological dad wasn't around much. He popped in and out of our lives. My mother used to let us stay with him for the summer and we cried to go back home. When we visited him in Mississippi, he was so strict with us. He didn't try to do anything to make a boring vacation fun. My mom and stepfather drove all the way from Florida to Mississippi just to pick us up.

I did not feel like me and my dad had a real bond. Our grandmother Joan always made sure she filled in the areas he lacked and kept us acquainted with their side of my family.

All I can remember is him wanting me to play football and follow in his footsteps. I liked football but I didn't have a passion for it. I didn't see myself going pro.

I was always a ladies' man. I had my first girlfriend in preschool. I broke up with her and got another girlfriend the same week because she was too mean. I was almost expelled from elementary school in kindergarten for sticking my hands down a girl's pants. My mom beat the living daylights out of me. She didn't understand that was my girlfriend! (Laughing out loud!)

I was easily bored in class because I was always the first one done with my schoolwork. In Kindergarten, I did second grade work with my sister Karesha. We were so competitive growing up. I wanted to do everything better than her and show her I was smarter. We played together and fought a lot - all in love. She is the definition of *my real day 1*.

Our mom got both of us into sports at the age of four and we were very active. I played football and baseball. My sister played softball and was a cheerleader. Naturally athletic, we grew up loving to play sports.

Playing baseball taught me how to be social and respect other races at a young age. For a majority of the seasons I played, I was the only black player on the team. If not the only, I was one of few. Always the fastest person on my team, I was the leadoff batter and played multiple positions - short stop, center field, and even sometimes pitcher. I knew I was a threat to the other teams, and they feared me, but for some reason I never made the all-star team.

When it came to football, I was always undersized, but I had a big heart. My first year playing flag football we won the Super Bowl. When I moved up to the tackle division, I was younger than most of the team, so I learned the game getting roughed up by older boys. Every time they hit me hard, I got back up and gained more confidence.

Youth football back then was worse than boot camp. The coaches ran us to *death*, as soon as we got to practice. If anyone was one minute late, they knew to start running and their tardiness increased the duration of the run. Our drills included hitting against the hardest hitters on the team. There was no way to *duck the smoke.*

It paid off and we won the Super Bowl my first year playing tackle. In fact, we became back-to-back Super Bowl Champs. I finally got to play

♪

with my age group. I made a lot of lifetime friends playing football.

At the age of seven, my stepfather was promoted to a better job, making more money, and he moved the family out of the projects. *We got a house y'all!* At this time, all the violence was frequently happening across town in the projects. We were happy to move away without knowing we were moving into an environment which would become worse.

In 1997 we moved to 1049 Hickory Lane Cocoa, FL 32922. This area was commonly called *North Fiske, Up-Town, Chocolate City.* I literally stayed across the street from the most dangerous apartment complex in the city, the *800s.*

I enrolled into Endeavor Elementary School in second grade. I was so anxious to go to school because most of my friends from my football team went there. We shared so many memories and learned various childhood lessons by going to Endeavor. It seemed like everyone was already grown. We knew everything the adults tried to keep away from us. We were street smart and book smart because of the environment we grew up in and our older siblings' influences. Our principal and teachers were like another set of parents. They *actually* disciplined us and beat us in front of the class. Then they called our parents and told them they did it. That's the kind of relationship we had.

Mrs. Watson was my favorite teacher. She was my teacher for 3rd, 4th, and 5th grade. Our principal, Mrs. Lyons was the coolest ever. She used to make sure we went on the best field trips – all the high-end theme parks people travel across the world to enjoy! You name it, we went there. We also had school dances every Friday night that were always *lit*. The older middle school kids came to our dances and *turned up.* Everybody used to dance back then, and we joked, "You wasn't really poppin' if you couldn't get a lap dance from the girl you crushed on."

Elementary was a fun experience. I had my first kiss and first fights, created my first clique and got my name. My cousin Chico C, my homeboy Tonio, and myself came up with a schoolhouse clique called CBS, "Can't Be Stopped". During sixth grade, we were the ones with all the motion on campus. All the ladies loved us, and all the fellas respected how we *were coming.* Everybody I hung out with should have been in middle school already, so our clique had the advantage.

Around that time, I started rapping and recording myself. The song, "Take It to The House" by Trick Daddy (Slip N Slide Records) was super-hot at the time. He said in the lyrics, "Hit me up Tray Plus dot com and tell me where you from." Ever since then, my homies started calling me Tray Plus. I ran with it, and it became my rap name. I entered talent shows often in elementary and loved rapping with my friends for fun.

By the time I hit eighth grade, I was the captain of my football team. Ask Coach Tony, he can tell you about my heart. When the competition came, I didn't join them, I went against them.

The skating rink was the spot every kid throughout the entire Brevard County linked up at. We skated, danced, fought, and did everything else there. Some nights we stayed from 7 pm to 7 am.

My mother and stepfather were never strict on my sister and me. We actually got to hang out and do whatever we wanted to do as long as we were behaved in school and made good grades. We got in trouble if we brought home a 'C'. I was always an 'A' honor roll student, so I was allowed to go to all the events.

Our movie nights were so *lit*. The whole theater was packed with a bunch of bad kids and no parental supervision. It used to be like a club inside of the theater.

We had big end of the year fights at a local park. Everybody packed eggs, whipped cream, and water guns filled with water and hot sauce. People really vandalized you if you were caught lacking.

Teen Fest, at the end of the year, was *the move* too. All the teenagers from the county linked up and partied all day and night at the venue.

There was major *beef* between some of the cities, so it often ended in a big brawl.

You had to be on your *Ps and Qs* growing up *outside* in the 90's-early 2000's. Anyone considered soft or sweet had *their card pulled* by the bullies. I wasn't in the house growing up, I was everywhere it was *swole* at.

# 3
# Off The Porch

<u>Summer 2004:</u>

Going into my freshman year of high school, I still hung out with some of my friends from elementary school. We went through middle school together and chose to go to Rockledge High. Even though we were from Cocoa, the next city over, most of my family went to Rockledge High. Since I previously played football for Rockledge Little League, I felt it was only right.

Cocoa and Rockledge have always been rivals. Once upon a time they were the same school until rezoning divided them up into two. Rockledge and Cocoa are adjacent cities in Florida. You can drive through both cities in less than twenty minutes. We all grew up together. The only difference we noticed is Rockledge doesn't have a hood. Anyone who lived in Rockledge and went to Rockledge High, we considered privileged. In contrast, it seemed like every corner you turn in Cocoa, there are *hoods* - a lot of low-income housing, apartments, and crime. I feel like they separated us on purpose. Any students I knew from single parent homes or those who received government assistance, most likely went to Cocoa High. Students who had parents with good jobs and were happily married, tended to be assigned to Rockledge High.

I was in an academic success program that helped prepare students for postgraduation. The advanced classes I took allowed me to go to Rockledge High even though I was considered out of area. My big sister Karesha was a Junior there. She drove to school, so I caught a ride with her.

Ninth grade I was always dressed to impress. Mom Dukes did her big one and I had a summer job. We used to wear all our clothes three sizes too big and the 2 for $89 Reebok classics were in style. One fresh white and one black pair, meant you were *stepping nice* for a few days.

Class was class, it was super boring so after we did our work, we freestyled. We made beats on the desk using our pencil and hands. I have always been into music.

I still had love for football, too. I tried out and made the freshman team. I started with the running back, cornerback, kicker, and kick return positions. After the first few weeks of practice, the coach noticed my advanced footwork, football IQ, and fell in love with my skills. He decided to start me on both sides of the ball.

Our first game of the season was a home game on the same field the varsity players utilized. I was super excited. I was set to start on offense and defense. During pregame warmups, a life changing event occurred. I goofed around and out of all the positions I was starting for; I chose to warm-up kicking the ball. After attempting to kick the ball, I felt something in my hip area pop. I thought one of my teammates threw a football tee and it hit me in my leg. I got up from the ground and asked, "Why y'all playing? Who threw that tee and hit me with it?"

My teammates replied, "Nobody threw anything at you. You trippin'!"

I got up and tried to walk it off and I couldn't. I fell to the ground. I told the coach what happened. He told me to sit out during the first half and if I felt better, I could start the second half.

When the second half came, Coach walked over to me and asked me to do a few running drills to see how I looked. I looked horrible. Coach saw the pain in my eyes every time I tried to make a cut, "Take your equipment off. You're not playing today."

I cried so hard because in my mind I already knew my season was over. After going to the doctor and getting X-rays, it was revealed that my hip was fractured. That injury canceled my freshman season, and I was heartbroken. I knew I messed up my chances of getting the varsity coaches' attention, making it almost impossible to make an impact on the football field. It was hard watching my friends play the remainder of the season and move up to the varsity roster. *That was supposed to be me*, frequently raced through my mind. I still question how my hip was fractured without any contact. I missed the entire season. I never played even one game.

When I eventually recovered, I tried out for the baseball team and made it. Once again, I was the only black kid on the baseball team. I was super fast and of course I knew the game I played my whole life. The coaches did not like me. I didn't have an equal opportunity to start. I barely got in the game and my love for baseball declined. I finished the season but that was my last year playing baseball. Freshman year was in the books.

Summer 2005:

Now fifteen years old, I passed the driver's test and received my learner's permit. My sister let me have her old car. In my mind I was grown. I was driving and had a job.

All my friends were already advanced. Some were having sex, smoking weed, skipping school, or all the above. I still tried to walk a straight path. I wanted to wait until marriage to have sex. That's something my mother always told us to do. I thought I would go to hell if I had sex before marriage, so I stuck to my mom's instructions. My friends Ken and Jae *clowned* me every day for being a virgin. When I got tired of them picking on me, I decided to test the water.

I didn't have a girlfriend at the time, and I wanted to lose my virginity that summer. So, we all snuck over to our classmate's house while her parents were at work. She liked all of us, so she let all of us have a turn. When it was my turn, I told her I was a virgin and had never done *it* before. I was nervous as hell. I knew she was super experienced because she used to skip class with the upperclassmen. *It* literally lasted 57 seconds (laughing my ass off). I came so fast; I didn't even realize I lost my virginity. After I was done Ken and Jae *clowned* me, but they were also happy for me. I was no longer a virgin. It wasn't the exact way I expected my first time to be, but I wouldn't change it.

Ken and I have been close friends since we were seven years old. I met Jae in 2004 at Teen Fest's end of the year bash. He moved to Florida from Texas during our ninth-grade year, and we became super tight. I introduced Ken and Jae to one another, and we all became close friends. Going into tenth grade all of us 'were in our bag with confidence on 1,000%'. We knew we were *them guys* on campus. Even the twelfth graders wanted us to hang around them. All the older females were choosing us. Ken and Jae ended up forming another group of friends who I wasn't interested in hanging out with, so we fell back from each other.

I started rapping more and more. I went home and told my mom I wanted to be a rapper. I asked her if she would help me get studio time. At this early stage, blowing up as a rapper was a slim chance to none. People were not giving local artists a chance. Anyone who wasn't on the radio or another media outlet was told to *hang it up*. My mom told me, "Get out of my face. I don't have no money for no studio."

That really upset me. I knew I had a real talent, but my mom didn't see it at the time. I made up my mind, *I'm going to make my own money.* During this period of time Young Jeezy dropped, "Thug Motivation"; TI dropped, "Urban Legend"; Rick Ross dropped, "Port of Miami"; and 50 Cent dropped, "Get Rich or Die Trying". These 2005 hits influenced me to get money and rap.

A group of us decided to start selling weed around the same time. There was no exotic weed back then, it was 'reggie' with sticks and seeds. We spent $60 on our first ounce and learned how to bag it up together - nickel, dime, and dub bags with no scale. It wasn't right if you didn't double your money. You should make $120 from $60 of product.

I remember buying my first ounce of weed one day before school. I had it in my bookbag the entire day. In Math class, everyone smelled it on me except the teacher. Luckily, I made it home and bagged it up. I was ready to start my new job in the morning. I spread the word around campus and things picked up for me.

My friend Ken was arrested and expelled for possessing cannabis on a school campus with intent to sell. That didn't stop me from hustling. My clientele grew and all my friends shopped with me. I had people spending $50 at a time. One day a friend from my football team came up to me as we walked to our next period. He asked, "Can I buy some weed off you?"

I responded, "How much do you want?"

He answered, "I have five dollars. Can you sell me a joint?"

"I don't sell joints. I got white boys spending $50 with me every time."

He didn't like the statement I made, "Man, that's messed up. I thought we was homeboys."

I felt sorry for him and ended up selling him a nickel bag. Without thinking anything of it, we went to our next class together. Toward the end of the class period, he asked the teacher, "May I be excused to go to the bathroom?" At the same time, he rummaged through his backpack, but no one expected anything.

The teacher excused him and let him leave class early to go to the restroom. The bell rang and everyone began switching classes. As we walked to our next class, people yelled, "Do y'all smell that? It smells like someone is smoking in the bathroom!"

We laughed at the craziness and continued in route to class. I never thought that was the same dude I sold the *nick'* to. *He was breaking down the swisher in class. He was the one smoking the weed in the bathroom.*

Sure enough, he got caught.

As I sat in class joking with my friends, the principal and the school resource officer walked through the door. The principal asked my teacher, "Do you have a Trashon Waller in your class?" As soon as I heard my name, I looked up puzzled wondering, *"What can he possibly want with me?"*

Once he saw my reaction, he knew it was me and never took his eyes off me, "Pack up your belongings and come with me."

He literally walked out of the classroom backwards so I wouldn't make any moves. Once we got into the office, the dreaded question came, "Where is the pot?"

*Yep, you got it right.* My so-called friend was caught smoking on campus and told the police everything. My principal knew I had more, and I had it on me. Both of us were arrested and expelled. Once I made it to the police station, they called the juvenile detention center to see if they had room for me. The officer said if my mom didn't come to the station before a bed was available, they would transport me.

My mom was notified. Quickly, she and my stepdad were in route to pick me up. While I sat in the holding cell, I thought about my rap career. I felt I had a story to tell.

My parents arrived and were allowed to take me home. My mom's eyes were red like she had been crying the whole ride to get me and my stepdad looked at me and shook his head. They were so upset; we went days without speaking.

Eventually, we talked about it, and I gave them my reasons for doing what I did. One of my consequences was to enroll in an alternative school. My friend Ken was already there, and we went through the same process. He gave me the whole run down and said not to worry.

I was fifteen years old with felony charges. I was ordered to go through a drug program, do community service, and maintain good grades. After I completed the drug program, I went to court and the judge expunged my record. My career as a young teenager rapper had begun.

# 4
# Fell In Love With Rap

After being released from the police station, all I wanted to do was tell my story. That's exactly what I did.

Oh Tray, it's okay. I know you messed up but I'm singing this song to our family. You was out there trying to make the littlest change then you ended up with a felony mane but we gonna pray for you Tray.

I thought of that chorus and instantly got on the phone with my cousin Si Weezie. Si and I grew up loving music, she always sang and danced as far back as I can remember. That was our first collaboration of many. She sang the chorus, and I rapped the verses. My delivery wasn't the best, but I actually told my story in detail. I spoke on the whole situation that occurred at school and the things I learned from it.

I let my family hear it and everyone was impressed. They kept making me play it over and over again every time a new family member walked in. That was the exact response I knew I would get. I felt my passion for music rapidly increasing. I bought a stick computer microphone from an electronics store, downloaded audio software, and I went to work.

I still couldn't believe I had been snitched on by my friend. On my first day at the alternative school, I was kind of nervous because I was now where all the *bad* kids went who were expelled. I was expecting there to be a lot of fights and a bunch of misbehavior going on all day. But instead, I found it to be a fun experience. My friend Ken and a lot of other friends who I grew up with were there as well. The work was super easy. It helped me bring my grade point average up further. I made straight A's every grading period.

After school Si came over to my house and we wrote and recorded music all night. I was never the normal teenage rapper. I was always explicit. I constantly used curse words and rapped about things beyond my age. I only rapped about things I went through or witnessed firsthand.

One day my friend Jae told me he was going to make a diss song about me. Jae and Ken became very close, and I was no longer cool with Jae. They formed their high school clique, and I didn't want any part of it. It became a competition, and we ended up talking to the same girls a lot. One particular girl played both sides and she added fuel to the fire. Jae's whole clique hated me.

Ken always made sure he made it clear he still had love for me. I'm the type of person who can't be cool with someone who hangs out with a bunch of people who envy me. Another member of Jae's clique, who had the most *pressure* with me, enrolled in the alternative school. We often almost fought right in the classroom. The only thing that stopped it from happening was me. I knew if I fought him in class I would be expelled from the alternative school, resulting in me having to repeat tenth grade again.

Jae still attended Rockledge High, so we rarely saw one another. He eventually came out with his diss track about me and sold me out big time. He spoke about me being snitched on and how I lost my virginity to a female we all *hit*. Then I responded back and told him it was me who introduced him to a lot of people in the hood and how his friends wouldn't be his friends if it wasn't for me. I also clowned him for how he sold his drugs, unable to make a profit. Our diss battle became the most talked about topic from Rockledge High to the alternative school to Cocoa High. It was my first time being in rap *beef* and I liked it.

I refused to back down. We wrote multiple songs that dissed one another. We threatened each other on one of the first online direct messaging services. We chatted about what we were going to do to each other when we met up. At this time, we were getting deeper in the *streets* and started being infatuated with guns.

Jae's mom saw our threatening messages and contacted my mom. Our parents couldn't figure out where all the animosity came from, knowing we were just best friends. They told us to stay away from each other if we couldn't get along. All that went in one ear and out the other. Jae's friends hyped him up because they wanted to keep the *beef* going between the two of us, like Biggie vs 2Pac. The whole city tried to get involved once they realized we had real *beef*. People came up to me to ask if I needed help. It got to the point it wasn't safe for Jae to hang out *Up-Town* anymore.

Jae showed up at my school and asked to fight me. We went to a close by park and fought. Jae threw the first punch. I ducked, then picked him up, and slammed him. We tussled on the ground until back up for each of us arrived. Jae tried to swing a few more times and missed. Ultimately, our friends broke us up. The whole time I laughed because I knew I wasn't seriously fighting him. I never threw one punch at Jae. I couldn't see myself harming someone I considered a friend. A dude from Jae's clique recorded the fight and edited the video to make it seem as if Jae beat me up. He cut out the whole beginning of the fight and I didn't like that. The *beef* between us lasted throughout high school and none of his girlfriends were safe. I ended up having sex with his high school sweetheart, the girl he was so in love with. That was the ultimate get back. It was crazy between the two of us.

Through the rap *beef*, I was perfecting my craft. I wrote three mixtapes in one month. Every day I recorded three to five songs. My mom would get mad at my cousin Si and I when we rapped loudly late at night. My mom told us to 'shut up all that cursing' plenty of times and made Si go home. I fell in love with making music. Even though the quality was horrible, I still made music.

I bought 100-packs of blank CDs and burned my CDs myself. I wrote the title of the mixtape on the CD with a permanent marker along with my name and Myspace address on it. I passed them out around school and in the streets. My fan base grew, and I solidified my name as a local rapper. People no longer called me Trashon or Tray. The name "Tray Plus" started ringing bells.

After I completed alternative school, I tried to return to Rockledge High, but the principal denied me. I was forced to enroll into Cocoa High. It wasn't a bad thing, actually I was really excited. Everyone knew me at Cocoa High. That's where a lot of friends from my neighborhood attended and that was my area school. In my opinion, Cocoa High was nothing like Rockledge High. Cocoa was a better fit for me. I felt free to be myself and everyone accepted it.

There was a rule which required transfer students to sit out a year before being allowed to play sports at their new school. I still practiced with the varsity team. Coach Wilk was very impressed by my diligence to train, knowing I couldn't play in the game. I still hung around the team and worked out in the gym with them. That was my junior year. I knew I didn't have a bright future in football. I wouldn't be able to see the field until my senior year.

That's when I began to take rap even more seriously. I got tired of recording in my room on that cheap microphone and knew it was going to take money to advance. My Auntie Erica was the head manager at a local fast-food restaurant. I was instantly able to get a job through her. I used all my money to buy school clothes and studio time.

The first time I ever went to a real studio was with Cat. Cat was my cousin Tee's boyfriend. He was the neighborhood's biggest dope boy at the time. He had the *flyest* cars, big chains, real diamonds in his mouth, and stayed well dressed. I was happy to be able to go to his studio. He was ten years older than me, so he was like a *big homie*. I used to go to his studio and press record for him while he *spit* his raps. In my head I thought, *I rap way better than him,* but I liked his style. He was a hustler first and an inspiring rapper second. I told him about my passion for music and that I wanted to rap in his studio. He let me get in and I was super nervous. I never heard myself rap through the studio headphones before and I froze up. I was disappointed in myself. I felt like I blew a big opportunity.

When I got home, I told myself: *If I ever get into that studio again, I'm going to be prepared.* I wrote so much music and I practiced my delivery over and over again. Sure enough, he invited me over to the house where he built the studio. I recorded three songs and did a feature with him all in the same night. Cat and his friends were impressed. He was so impressed he wanted me to be a part of his label *Real Life Empire*. I was down for it all, anything to spend more time in the studio, feeding my passion to make music.

I never signed any papers or received any money from him. It was just an agreement bound by loyalty. I was his young prodigy. I snuck into clubs and hit the stage with him while he performed. I went city to city with him *grinding*. I helped pass out CDs, hung up posters, and went to events. The whole time I worked with him, he was so focused on his own rap career that he didn't realize he had a young star following him around. In the beginning, he picked me up and took me to the studio. After a couple of times, he became less interested in picking me up. When I called him a few times to ask, "Can I get in the studio today?" He told me he was coming to get me and then never showed up. It got to the point where I felt like I was begging to be a part of his movement, so I stopped calling.

After that I met Shube. Shube was a *super-dope* singer and songwriter who I met at the age of sixteen. Someone recommended I should book studio time with him instead of begging Cat for it. So, I booked my first session. I kid you not, I recorded six songs, all in three hours. Shube was impressed with my work ethic at such a young age. We bonded quickly and I ended up recording my first tape at his studio - sixteen songs. I used some of the industry artists' beats and I downloaded some off the internet. I didn't get this tape mastered but it sounded way better than it did when I recorded in my room.

I still collaborated with my cousin Si Weezie and I linked up with my friend Detee. Detee was always the best male singer in our hood. We grew up in the projects together, so we already had a bond. Once we started making music together, he became my big bro. The three of us spent a lot of time in the studio, making hit after hit. I formed my label at the age of sixteen, *Thumbs Up Entertainment.* I knew someone had to be in charge of releasing my music, so I thought of a company. *Thumbs Up* represents *Up-Town* and good music. Si became my first lady and Detee was the R & B singer. We did shows together, passed out CDs together, and we made a name for ourselves together.

Eventually, everyone at school knew me as a rapper. My teachers even knew I was rapping. I became popular on Myspace. Myspace was a social media website before Facebook. We had to log in to Myspace from a desktop computer. This was before smart phones. A Myspace page could be designed however the user wanted it, including adding music. It became one of the fastest ways to build a network that reached a lot of people at once. I was super smart with computers back then and could encode. I posted my music everywhere and set it on autoplay. It was under people's pictures, in their comments, and even on their profile page. There was no escaping it. I intentionally made sure people heard my music and my fanbase grew fast. *I had real fans.* Girls even changed their background images and put my picture there. I was number one on so many people's top eight friends. Girls used to send me pictures with my name signed on their boobs. I was becoming a hot commodity.

# 5
# Underdawg

My junior year of high school, I no longer cared for school. I came to class without a backpack and still passed because I'm smart. I could do whatever I wanted to, as long as I kept my grade point average above a 2.0, which was the eligibility requirement to play sports and graduate. I was a student with a 3.0 GPA with no plans of going to college. I made up my mind I wanted to be a rapper. I knew I had the formula to make it. At this time, there were no other teenagers taking rap seriously where I'm from. Soulja Boy was just starting to *blow up* on Myspace. I witnessed his whole come up. I stayed on my *grind* doing the same stuff he did, minus the dancing. I made a YouTube channel and started vlogging my life. I had real fans, but I was still being underestimated.

My experiences in Brevard County taught me people really must be *won over* to support someone. At this time, Iceburg Tony was the hottest artist in the county. He encompassed the total package. He had the lyrics, he had the image, and he had the *streets*. Iceburg Tony, Buddy Rowe, and Dreal had the county on lock when it came to music. I was a lot younger than them but they motivated me to go harder. I couldn't wait until it was my turn to have the club *rocking* like them one day. That became a goal of mine, so I kept making music.

Things changed at home. My mom caught my stepfather cheating and kicked him out of the house. My sister went off to college, so that left just my mother and I, in the heart of the hood. We used to argue a lot because I saw things differently and I was becoming a man. My mom wanted me to go to college and I hated school. I felt it served me no purpose in the real world. At the time, no one believed anyone from Cocoa, FL could make it as a rapper. The odds and the opposition are what made me want to take my ambition to be a rapper more seriously. I love making music and I love challenges. I knew I had to turn everyone into believers including my mother.

In my free time, I gambled with older dope boys. We played video games and competed for thousands of dollars. My homeboy D Murda and I were Madden freaks, so we were all in. We bet our fast-food worker paychecks on ourselves and came back home with more money. Everyone knew I was trying to rap but they always compared me to older rappers. To them, I was at a disadvantage. But I knew I had a key advantage. I knew if I kept *grinding* my time would come. I tried to perform at every big event for free. My heartfelt desire was for my music to be heard. I wasn't even eighteen years old yet and stood in front of big crowds of adults putting on shows at clubs. One by one people started to love my presentation. As I gained favor with the adult crowd, I still promoted my music within my age group. I knew the older rappers weren't targeting my age group or the generation under me. I was eager to pursue every opportunity to grow my audience. I advanced from opening up shows to being paid by the promoter anywhere from $250-$500. It wasn't much but I was thankful to be noticed and get paid doing what I love.

My senior year of high school, I was known as a rapper on campus, but my friends still treated me like a regular person. It was my teachers and principals who saw me as a future star. I remember walking into English class and my teacher greeted me at the door, "There goes my little rap star." That really stuck with me because I had people in one ear who told me *it's impossible*, then in the other ear I had her tell me *I got it*.

I made the varsity football team and started on both sides of the ball in the first game of the season. I played cornerback and slotback on offense. Coach Wilk saw *something* in me, being that I won first place in the weightlifting competition over the summer and was at every practice. Eventually, it became too hard to learn two playbooks when my heart was really in music. I lost both of my positions as a starter and became a role player in one of Cocoa High School's legendary football teams.

This was Coach Wilk's second year as head coach and Cocoa High's first year as regional champs. Our team was called "Dirty Thirty". We only had thirty players, but winning passion and the heart to persevere were both there. We played on the road against some of the toughest teams in Florida and won.

We lost the game scheduled right before state. It was a historical game because we were the *underdawgs*. We played Naples High School. It seemed like they had two teams to our one. They had a full roster, and everyone looked like they belonged in college. With over two thousand fans in the stands, we vowed *not* to be blown out. We never gave up. We fought hard and made a great comeback. We lost 28-21. So many tears shed on the field that night. We knew we were making history game-by-game and felt it was supposed to end with us winning state. Naples High ended up winning the state championship the next game by a blowout. We knew *if* we had beaten Naples High, we would have been champions. All the underclass players on our team experienced the feeling of a tough loss. That made them hungry and determined to win state and they did. They actually won the state championship three times in a row after that loss.

I graduated from Cocoa High School in May of 2008. It was a special moment I will never forget. My grandfather was there to see me walk across the stage before he died from cancer two months later. The way he battled with cancer for years before actually dying lets me know I come from a strong family. I even witnessed a time my grandfather died and came back to life. I take my grandfather's strength with me everywhere I go. I have his name, birthday, and homegoing date tattooed on my arm. I felt like he wanted to see me make a big accomplishment in my life before he physically left. I was voted CHS's class of 2008 "Most Likely to Become Successful".

# 6
# Boss Mentality

<u>2008</u>

After graduating high school, I dove back into the *streets* headfirst. I started selling better quality weed and I gained a solid clientele. My goal wasn't to get into the *streets* to build a reputation as a drug dealer. I knew my purpose and I stuck with it. I knew those $200 fast food restaurant payroll checks were not enough to push myself as an artist independently. No one believed in me enough to invest into me, so I had to create my own budget.

Every dollar I made I invested back into my career. I recorded my first official mixtape titled *Money & Musik*. I paid for the studio time and for every track to be mixed and mastered. I also paid for my outfit, a photoshoot, the CD cover artwork, and I duplicated 1,000 physical CDs. My confidence in this project was at an all-time high. The substance was there, the delivery was there, and the quality was there. I had the image, and I was hungry.

I broke up with my high school sweetheart that summer. I was 100% committed to getting money and my music career. That mentality influenced me to name my official mixtape *Money*

& *Musik.* I flooded the internet and the streets. I passed out my CDs city to city. My friends and I bum-rushed the local high schools as soon as the bell rang for dismissal. We made sure each kid we encountered got a CD. I hung up posters at every convenience store in the county and left CDs at the front counter for customers to grab for free. I wasn't chasing the money I just wanted my music to be heard.

Next thing I knew, I heard more people playing my music and more promoters reached out to me. PC and Brian "BG" Goins were the first promoters to pay me and let me showcase my talent. Once I bought an outfit and shoes for the show that money was gone so it still felt like I was doing it for free. I wasn't mad at them for paying me what they felt I was worth. I took it as motivation.

My goal was not only to pack the club. I wanted to rent the club for the night just like the promoters. I saw how much money they made in one night and it inspired me. I was advanced when it came to getting money.

I taught many of my friends how to sell drugs. We *trapped out* my homeboy's roommate's apartment, who became my everyday homeboy along with D Murda. D Murda stayed in the next building over, we've been *click tight* since middle school. We all became brothers. Everybody had NFL dreams except me.

I told my homies if they really wanted to be in the NFL then that's what they should be dedicated to. I knew I wanted to be a rapper so that's all I did. I rapped and I *trapped* knowing I needed the money to sponsor my career. I still worked out a lot because I wanted to have sex appeal and females to admire my image. My homeboys didn't get any D1 offers, maybe a few small schools were interested but nothing major. They ended up staying home and working fast food jobs and *trapped* on the side.

*Trapping* was my full-time occupation, so I took it more seriously than them. I was never in the *streets* for attention. I did what I had to do to get where I wanted to be. My mixtape didn't feature outsiders. I stuck with my *day ones*, Si Weezie and Detee. I wrote the entire mixtape myself. I stayed in *my bag* and wrote three to five songs daily. We all *linked up* in Hawthorn Apartments or hung out at Si's house in Candlewood Apartments. My phone rang so much I ended up *trapping out* another *crib* too.

When it was time for a show, we all met at Si's house for the pregame. We drunk, smoked, joked, and rehearsed our songs so we would be on point. My homie Reggie wasn't a rapper, but he knew all my lyrics. He was super hyper, so I started

♪

calling him *Hypeman.* We all became more of a family, and it started to feel like a label. My mom started to see how seriously I took my career and all the good feedback I received about my music. I no longer wanted to talk business for myself when it came to money matters, so I made my mom my manager. I taught her everything I learned and used her as my voice. When people called to book me or had inquiries, she was the person to speak to.

# 7
# Becoming a Father

I still remember like it was yesterday. My friend *Hypeman Reggie Reg* came up to me super excited while we were posted in the trap. He proceeded to tell me how he *ran down on a baddie* and that she was *messing with him heavy*. She also had a sister who would love to meet me and didn't believe Reggie and I were really friends. I reminded him I was fresh out of a relationship and was not interested in *messing* with anyone. Then I said, "But if she about that life, I will see what's up."

"Bro, all this girl do is listen to your music, she is a fan of yours. You gonna *hit* trust me," *Hypeman* replied.

So, I told him to set it up. The girls lived a few doors down from our *trap* with their older sister who worked a lot, leaving them home alone. Later that night we went to the girls' house to hang. *Hypeman* introduced me to everyone, and we started *vibin'*. The whole time we were *chilling* the girl *Hypeman* said was *messing with him heavy* didn't give him any *play*. She actually had another one of my homeboys come over and went into another room with him.

I spent my time getting to know the girl's sister. We stayed up all night, got high, and watched movies. I wanted to see what she was really about, so I tried to have sex with her on the first night. No matter how much I worked to get her in the mood she was not going for it. The sun eventually came up. I told her I needed to go home and get some rest. The fact that she wasn't down to have sex with me right away really made me respect her more because I would never wife someone who I *hit* the first night. When I got home, I received a text from her:

> I really enjoyed you and I wanted to have sex with you so bad. My period was on but the next time we hang out you can get it.

I can't lie, I started *feeling* myself. I knew she wasn't lying about anything she texted. The next time we hung out we had sex just like she said. Our first time having sex, the condom popped. I pulled out and I was shocked because I never expected to have *raw* sex with her. She wasn't an ugly looking girl, and she was cool, so I continued *chilling* with her.

If I wasn't *trapping,* I was a few doors down with her at her sister's house. She was a senior in high school, she ran track, she had a job, and she had a car. In all my nineteen years of living, up to this point, I never experienced a female doing all the above and that made me want her more. We grew feelings for one another and started letting each other into our personal lives. At that time, she and her mom were not on good terms, and she vented to me about it. Basically, she took care of herself while she tried to figure out what her life would be like after graduation.

I barely went home to my mom's house. I either slept in the *trap* or stayed the night with her. She reminded me that I gave her a CD while she was working at a restaurant in the area. That's how she first heard my music. She was intrigued and continued to listen a lot, especially while doing homework. She saw the superstar potential in me and was a real supporter.

She often brought food home from work and made sure I ate. It was the little things I respected about her that made me want to take our relationship further. I remember when I kissed her in the middle of the club, and it shocked her. Then I told her, "Now we go together." After three months of *talking,* we became an official couple.

My twentieth birthday was approaching. For some reason I always had it in my head that I wouldn't make it to see twenty. I wanted to make sure I had a child to carry my legacy. I told her that I wanted her to have my baby. She agreed and I started leaving *it* in every time on purpose. I promised her I would be a great father. She promised me she would never be a bitter baby's mother who gets mad and puts me on child support.

2010

She eventually got pregnant around my twentieth birthday. I was super excited to be a father. She was scared to tell her mom she was pregnant. I took all the money I had and got us an apartment in Melbourne, FL. I stopped selling drugs and we both got jobs. Money wasn't coming in fast, but we were able to pay our bills, our house was fully furnished, and we kept groceries.

I knew the 9 *to 5 life* wasn't really for me, but I made the change for my new family. I was at every doctor's appointment and every ultrasound. Once she realized she had me, she started acting like she could control me. Yes, I was trying to live a normal life, but I knew I was still *Tray Plus*. I knew I had to interact with my fans and be a *people person*. She used to get mad at me and try to tell me I can't communicate with my supporters. When she met me, she knew I had a lot of people supporting me and was all for it. I never stepped out on her, we literally spent our whole day together in another city. I couldn't understand why building my fan base and pursuing my career was a problem.

She had morning sickness really bad and couldn't keep any food down. It got to the point where our baby was underweight. We argued about her eating habits even though my intention was only to make sure she ate. We never argued before the pregnancy. Things changed super-fast. She became very abusive and felt like she could put her hands on me. I felt unappreciated. I literally stopped hustling in the *streets*, cold turkey. I got a job and secured us a place to stay. I was expecting peace and happiness, but our reality was the complete opposite.

Within ninety days of living there, I quit my job and made up my mind that it was best for us to move back to Cocoa. We needed to be closer to where the help was. I didn't pay to break the lease, I just packed up everything and left, which marked both of our credit reports with an eviction.

She eventually told her mom that she was pregnant and moved in with her. I also moved back in with my mom. From the first time I met my baby's mother, she and her mom didn't see eye to eye. Once her mom found out she was pregnant, they became close again.

When I moved back in with my mom, I jumped back out into the *streets*. This time I had more of a strategic plan. I knew what kind of money I needed to make and what I wanted to do with the money. No more hustling in apartment complexes. I was mobile, or I had my folks *pull up* on me. My baby's mother and I eventually got back together then she moved in with us. She was pregnant with my mother's first grandchild. My mom has always been a great supporter and does not *play* when it comes to her grandkids.

December 21, 2010, my daughter Azaria Tranae Waller was born. My baby's mother underwent an emergency C-section because the umbilical cord was wrapped around my daughter's neck causing her oxygen level to drop. She ended up being very small, 5 pounds 6 ounces but she wasn't premature. She was very healthy and very alert. She wasn't crying at all; she looked around and was very observant. That day I told my baby, "You will grow to become a star, and I promise I will be there every step of the way."

# 8
## Put Myself Last

My baby's mother and my daughter were cleared to go home from the hospital. My baby's mother was on bed rest for two weeks and in pain from the emergency C-section. I was completely new to this, but I was in full-time daddy mode. I was up late nights and early mornings taking care of our child while making sure my baby's mother didn't have to move around much. That allowed her to get the necessary rest to heal properly. I bathed my daughter, fixed bottles, changed diapers, and read her books.

Once my baby's mother was healed, all I wanted to do was catch up on my rest and get back on my *grind*. I didn't have an ordinary job; hustling was my job. I couldn't be in the house all day, every day, I had to provide. I basically started over from scratch with no clientele and a new phone. I knew I had major responsibilities now that my daughter was born. I didn't have anyone to invest in me. I had to *grind* to pay bills, take care of my daughter, and try to push my rap career all out of my pockets.

It was hard for me because every time I got focused, my baby's mother called to ask for something. I'm far from a deadbeat and I would do

♪

anything for my child. I was trying to get my baby's mother to understand my money wasn't my money and I had to reup to keep *business* going. When she randomly asked me for money it would throw my whole *grind* off. I kindly told her if she needed anything from me to please let me know in advance because money was tight, and every dollar was accounted for. Instead of her supporting my *come up* she called me a deadbeat and said I don't do anything for my child. In reality, my child had her own room at our house with a closet full of everything she needed. My daughter never went without.

Despite us staying at my mom's house our relationship became even more toxic. She was still very unappreciative and seemed to like having physical altercations with me. She didn't care who was around at the moment. We argued in front of my homeboys, and we even argued around my mom. We eventually broke up again and she moved back in with her mom. Then she went against everything she promised me. My daughter was three months old when I received those child support papers. I went a few months without seeing my own child because my baby's mother kept her away from me. She claimed her mom made her put me on child support to receive government assistance.

Next thing I knew, she had a new boyfriend who was at the time wanted for murder. It seemed like everything she possibly could do to throw me off my *grind* she did, and it always involved my daughter. If it wasn't for my daughter, she would be a nonfactor. I never gave a female that many chances to play with me. I fought through it all because I never imagined my kid not living under the same roof as me. She wrongly thought I was fighting for her love, but I was fighting to keep our family together.

I eventually got focused again on my *grind*. My mom's house became my *trap* spot. I ate, slept, and *trapped* there. My mom knew what I was doing but she saw how I moved and trusted me. She was more comfortable with me being at home than in the streets.

I trained my pit bull as a puppy to be a guard dog. He warned us if anybody walked on our property. I never served anyone who just showed up at my house. People knew to call me first, then I came outside to serve them. I stopped serving after 10 pm. It wasn't because I was scared, I just didn't want traffic coming to my house late at night.

I ran my money up and got back to music. As I was becoming the hottest young rapper in my county, I decided to shine my light on my peers. I always had an ear for talent, and I never was a hater. At twenty years old, I had six other artists under my label. I put all my solo missions to the side and focused on everyone else. I felt we all could make it and I had the route. I knew we didn't have a big budget but if we all put in the effort it could blow the whole label up.

I used to have to beg people to record music. I thought everyone wanted to be rappers and singers. Really, everyone wanted the attention rappers and singers got. Once some of the artists started getting a *buzz* in the *streets* their work ethic declined. Folks stopped showing up to the fundraisers and started being late to the label meetings. Some artists even jumped ships. They wanted to go where they *thought* their career would be more promising.

A few artists left my label to join another label thinking just because the CEO had money that would boost their career. I knew it took more than money. Great marketing and a solid promotion plan are necessary. That was the part I had, but what I was missing was the big money. I dropped the artists who wanted to leave and kept the ones who wanted to stay.

I dropped another compilation mixtape. Instead of seven of us, we were down to four. At twenty-one years old, I ran my label all by myself. I booked label photoshoots, released the mixtape, and booked the clubs myself. People saw what I was trying to do but they *hated on* me instead of getting behind me and supporting me.

People even opposed me by going on the internet to influence others not to come to my events. They knew I paid thousands of dollars to rent the club out myself and they didn't want to see me pack it out. Dudes literally threatened their girlfriends and told them they better not go support me. I took many losses. I booked the club and barely anybody showed up. I literally invested all the money I had into the event thinking everyone would come out and support. I woke up the next day drunk and broke.

After trying to make the group thing work for the second time I decided to focus on my solo career again. I got back on my *grind* and started saving up my money. I'm big on trying to get the best quality out of my music. I desired to record where the stars recorded. I researched a recording studio named Patchwerk in Atlanta, Georgia. Many big celebrities stopped through to record their albums there and I wanted to do the same. I booked a studio session and took a trip to Atlanta by myself. I paid $1,400 for one song titled, 'All About My Come Up'. That was the first song I had all exclusive rights to. I paid the producer $400 for the beat, $500 for studio time, and another $500 to get it professionally mixed and mastered. When I got home, I paid another $500 to shoot the video.

I paid to get *All About My Come Up* t-shirts made and handed them out for free. I booked the club once again and told everyone I was shooting a music video. I got the same results; a lot of folks didn't come. That was $2,000 gone down the drain.

Nevertheless, I can't necessarily say I wasted the money because we did end up shooting the video and captured good content. I was just *broke* again the next day. My baby's mother and her friends were in the video. She played the main model role and let me use some of her money to stunt like rappers do. My family and a few friends showed up to support me. Jae was one of those friends. We eventually squashed our high school *beef* and started supporting each other again. I dropped the *All About My Come Up* music video and everyone started realizing my quality was unmatched. I had the *hardest* local video out at the time and my song sounded like it belonged on the radio. I couldn't fully promote the project how I wanted to because I spent all the money I had to make it happen and I didn't get any money in return when I booked the club.

Back to square one, hustling to get my money back up. I served all the big-time dope boys. My big bro Diddy was one. He spent hundreds of dollars with me each day. When I told him about everything I had going on and how everyone tried to sabotage my vision, he felt my pain. We decided to put our brains together and come up with a solution. Instead of me spending all my money on the events, big bro decided to book the club for me. I knew the adult crowd wasn't my crowd, but at that time I took too many losses dealing with haters. I told big bro Diddy, "Let's do it, I got a plan!"

Summer 2012:

At the age of twenty-two, I was like a big brother to many of the teens. There were a lot of shootings, car thefts, and burglaries going on and the teenagers were the ones committing most of the crimes. Older people were terrified of these kids.

I knew in my heart the kids were mainly acting out because they weren't given the attention they needed, and they didn't have anything to look forward to. That's when I came up with KMAFT (Keep Me Away From Trouble). I told big bro Diddy about the plan, and we started doing events for the teens instead of the adults. Our first event was a huge success. We packed out the club and there was no drama at all. Big bro made his money back and we split the profits. There wasn't much of a profit, but it was more than what the promoters previously paid me, and it was for a good cause. We only charged the teens $5-$15 to get in and they had a ball.

Our next event was a Sunday Funday Beach Party and the after party was at the club. Both events were a success, and we were making a huge impact in these kids' lives. I wanted to give them everything the older people held back from giving me. We had rap battles and dance contests for cash prizes. We put many young inspiring artists on stage for the first time in their lives, giving them an opportunity to showcase their talents in front of three hundred plus peers.

My big bro Diddy ended up catching a Fed case and was sentenced to ten years in prison. I was back hustling on my own. I was getting *hot* in the *streets* and the police started to watch my house every day. They made it hard for me to make money. One officer literally parked in front of my house and stayed there all day. When that happened, I packed my bags and moved myself to Atlanta. I had an older homeboy who lived there and told me he could help put me in position. He wanted me to sell weed for him, but I knew that wasn't what I was trying to do. I figured if he had enough money to front me weed, he had enough money to help my music career take off.

He thought I was coming to get some weed from him, but I already had it in my mind I wasn't coming back to Cocoa, FL. I packed about ten outfits and a few pairs of shoes then hopped on the bus. Yes, I left my car at home to get repossessed and took the bus to Atlanta.

In the back of my mind, I knew this dude was a fraud and there was a chance I was going to get left stranded. I had $250 and a bunch of CDs to my name. I already made a *survival* plan if he wasn't willing to help me. I *hit him up* to let him know I was getting off the bus and he did exactly what I felt he was going to do. He ignored me and left me stranded.

My plan was to get a cheap motel room and *grind* my CDs every day until I made enough money to get another room and put a little money into savings.

One of my classmates by the name of Tek *hit* me in my *DM* and let me know he lived in Atlanta and if I needed anything to *hit* him up and that is exactly what I did. I told him about how I came to Atlanta and was stood up by my so-called partner and was *crashing* at a motel until I got myself together. He volunteered for me to come stay with him for a few months if I needed to. It was so cold that night and I was ready to leave the cheap motel. I asked him to come *scoop* me. Thankfully, he came expeditiously.

# 9
# Sacrifice

Tek welcomed me into his *crib*. He was going through a divorce, so it was just us living on the outskirts of Atlanta, in a country city called Loganville, Georgia. There wasn't any *motion* out there for me. Tek had a good job, and I was desperately looking for a job. With no car, I was stuck and stranded in the house a lot. We lived one hour away from the city and Tek didn't want me to put a lot of miles on his car. I appreciated Tek for giving me a place to stay when I had nothing to offer. I applied for food stamps and was approved, so I started putting groceries in the house. I felt that was the least I could do to show homie I wasn't trying to leach off him.

We went to a few events, I even performed at an open mic. We went to a mansion party and Tek gave me a few dollars to throw on the strippers. He's a real one and I salute him for that.

Tek gained the upmost respect from me when my lil brother got kicked out of his girl's crib and he let him stay with us. My younger blood brother, on my daddy's side, was staying in Atlanta at the time too. We all became brothers and started *vibin' tough*.

Lil bro and I were stuck in the house while Tek was at work. It became frustrating and overwhelming for both of us. My little brother never had our dad in his life either, so we always shared our resentment. We decided we couldn't live with Tek any longer and that it was time to go back to Florida. I have never been the type of person to live off the next man, stranded with no car. I had to make a move.

Before I left, I wrote a business plan. Inside the plan I detailed my goals for a year. I planned to go home and turn my record label into a legit business. I wanted to release music, come out with my clothing line, and shoot a music video advertising the *merch*. I researched and listed all the prices for everything I needed in my business plan.

I printed out roughly ten copies of my plan. My strategy was to approach successful OGs and local businesses at home. I made Tek my business partner. I felt like it was only right being that he went out of his way for me while I was in Georgia.

Once I made it back to Florida, I approached a few local businesses, barbershop owners, and OGs who had *bank*. I asked a lot of people to invest in my vision. Only two people cared enough to give a donation. Zee from Fresh Street (a clothing store) gave me $50 and the owner of the 800's hair store gave me $25. That really meant something to me.

The fact that these two men were not originally from Cocoa, FL and are a different race than me stood out.

The barber who cut my hair every week read my plan and didn't give me a dollar. One of my OGs I used to talk business with read my business plan and didn't give me a dollar. When the majority overlooked me, two people gave me what they could, and I appreciated it. Though it wasn't much numerically, those $75 are a significant part of my history. I had a plan and $75 to my name.

I knew I had to start back hustling. This time I had a clearer plan of how to become a bigger businessman and artist. I grabbed a quarter ounce of exotic weed with the $75 and sold $15 grams. I made $105 back and bought another quarter the same day. When I went to reup again, later that day, I bought a half, and my homie *fronted* me with the other half. I went from a quarter ounce to an ounce in one day. I didn't smoke anything; I needed every dollar. If I did smoke, it was because I took a point off each gram. By the time I bagged up ten grams I had a free gram to smoke. No one ever noticed or complained about being short .1 gram.

I was solely focused on my *grind* and every-one knew it. Still, nobody gave me any money, but I had respect in the *streets*. My face was *clean*. Everybody with *weight* knew they could give it to me, and I would sell it with no problems. I no longer had to invest all my money. Every time I bought weed people *fronted* me more. It got to the point where I was able to *front* my homeboys to help them get on their feet. Money was coming in and I was getting closer to my goals.

Tek ended up resigning from his job and moved back to Florida. At this time, things were hard for him, and he didn't have extra money to invest into the business. I remembered all the things he did for me while I was in Georgia. I decided to invest all my money into the business and still make it seem like he was helping. I told him I had a plan, and it was going to take off, just be patient.

We relaunched the KMAFT teen nights. The first event Tek and I put together was a back-to-school bash. We went to the store and filled a cart up with all kinds of school supplies. Even though I was the only one who invested, I still took a picture with Tek in front of the shopping cart. I booked the venue, and paid for security, DJs, and advertisements. It was a success; we packed roughly 400 kids in one building. We had a rap battle for cash prizes and passed out school supplies. During the whole event I had Tek with me front and center. I kept his image intact and made it seem like he helped me put it all together when in reality it was my plan and my funds. I never told anyone about it, I thought we were going to rise together.

Eventually, Tek started feeling some type of way towards me. We began to *bump* heads a lot. I felt like he didn't expect me to be able to come home and do everything I said I was going to do without help.

My first clothing brand I released was called YFR (Youngest Freshest Realest). I spent $1,500 on *merch* and gave it all away for free. I booked a club for my video shoot and party, models for the photoshoot, a hotel suite, and a rental truck. I spent one thousand dollars on my outfit. I was invested into the vision. Once again, I had Tek right with me as if he was helping financially. I came out with the clothing brand, a music video, and a DVD. I couldn't believe it, I actually had people buying my *merch* and DVDs. The animosity between me and Tek grew, the more focused I became. He was going through his own personal issues and was trying to get his life back in order. I wanted him to focus more on the business, but I couldn't force him, so we ended up going our own separate ways.

I eventually tried to make things work again with my baby's mother. Her older cousin let her rent out her house which was around the corner from my mother's house. I spent a majority of my nights there with her and my daughter. I tried to ignore the fact she put me on child support and literally took me through hell. I just wanted to be the best father to my child. I thought being there in the same house was the answer, but it wasn't.

One night I decided to go through her phone while she was asleep to see who she had been talking to. I ran across my homeboy Tek's name. I read a message from him telling her to come get some money to get her hair done and there were many others, definitely enough evidence to conclude they communicated on a regular basis. I tapped her cheek so hard. I wouldn't say I slapped her, but it was hard enough to wake her up. I showed her the messages and a fight erupted. She acted like she was the one who deserved to be mad and kicked me out of her house. After that day I knew there was no future between us. I never let Tek know I read his messages. I stopped dealing with him completely.

This same year my homeboy D Murda married his high school sweetheart, and I was his best man. A few months later our friendship came to an end. Our visions no longer aligned, and we argued too much. He knew his NFL dreams were dead and I was still chasing my high school dream. I felt like he didn't believe in me, and he wanted me to lose my self-confidence. Any time I spoke about my goals, it seemed like he tried to crush them. I told him and our friend *Hypeman* Reggie I had to cut them off. I don't like arguing with people, especially when they're trying to devalue me and convince me to stop *grinding* towards my dreams.

2013

I made life changing sacrifices in order to get to the next level. I broke up with my baby's mother for good and ended my closest friendships. It hurt me deeply. I weighed every bit of 129 pounds around this time. I felt like everyone I showed genuine love to, gave me their butts to kiss. The people I believed in and held to high standards left me for dead. I became distant from everyone and got closer to the inner God.

I prayed more and asked God for guidance. I needed Him to remain in my corner as I tried to escape my past. I spent a lot of time with my daughter, teaching her how to use her brain. I showed her how to be an entertainer and *not* to be camera shy. I was one-on-one, hands on with my daughter. I instilled in her the knowledge and fundamentals she needs in order to advance beyond her peers. I sat down with a lawyer and *Thumbs Up Music Group* became an LLC and I became a CEO.

Once I cut off all the distractions and negativity things started to flourish for me. I packed out teen nights and adult nights. On my twenty-fourth birthday I had a radio interview and

I paid for my hit single, *Blame It On My Old Girl,* to get in rotation. I threw my annual Aries Ball and packed the club out. Everybody came out to support me. I rolled up twenty-eight blunts of exotic and bought a lot of bottles. I passed out free blunts and liquor to my people to show my appreciation to the packed-out crowd. I reflected on the times when nobody showed up for me. Once I removed who I *thought* I needed in my life and started listening to God more, things started to blossom for me. I was becoming the next big star out of Florida.

# 10
# Death Row

A part of me wanted to focus on my solo career, then another part of me wanted to bring the homies with me. I put a lot of hard work into my craft and people were starting to see it pay off for me. A lot of my friends started rapping for fun and I saw potential in them. We were hustlers first so money wasn't an issue. I came up with a bright idea to bring all of us together. I knew if we used our *muscle* in the *streets* with my knowledge in music we could take off.

Jae and I started *kicking* it again on a regular basis like we used to. Ken came home from a prison bid. My homie Boo, who pulled up on me to buy weed every day, let me hear some of his raps and I was very impressed. Boo and I go way back. Boo, Ken, and I played on the same little league football team in the 90's and we also went to school together. I told him that Ken and Jae were already *down* and we wanted him to be a part of the movement. He liked the idea, and we planned a meeting for all of us to *link up* and hangout.

We went to Miami to celebrate our first time *linking* as one. We knew the power of unity and were ready to take over the *streets*. Jae and Ken had their people behind them, I had my people behind me, and Boo had his people behind him.

We were like the Hot Boyz in the early 2000s. There was so much hype around us because we were still in the *streets* - hustling and making a lot of money.

We rented office space and made it our own recording studio. We recorded and *trapped* all day in that spot. That was our life. We realized we needed to come up with a group name. I was *Thumbs Up*, Ken and Jae were *Black Code*, and Boo was *800 Bound*. Once we became a whole, we started calling ourselves the new *Death Row*.

We knew what we brought to the game was authentic and we were not like most rappers. We lived what we rapped about, and we wanted to bring back real *street* music. We released our first demo titled, "All For One, One For All." All four of us were featured on the cover. We grew a buzz so fast that we were invited as special guests to Lil Boosie's welcome home concert in Daytona. The whole city now saw the potential we had. We elevated to the point where other dudes wanted to be a part of our group. Rappers started coming to our studio to record. Those who came consistently, we eventually welcomed into our new *Death Row*.

We knew we didn't want any legal problems with our group's name down the line, so we decided to spell it differently. Instead of *Death Row* we called ourselves *Deaf Row Hit Squad*. We became deaf to all the negativity, without knowing it was knocking on our front door. We threw our demo release party at a local club in Cocoa and packed it out. The whole county came out to support us. We performed our songs from the demo, and we gave other artists under our group a chance to showcase their talent. It was a success. We booked the club ourselves, so all the door money was ours. We made over $7,000 that night.

Now that we saw we could bring a crowd we jumped into the club promotion lane. We paid $10,000 to bring YFN Lucci to Central Florida for the first time of his career. At that time YFN Lucci was just catching a *buzz* with his first mixtape, "Wish Me Well". I told the group he would be next *up*, and we needed to book him fast before a bigger city like Orlando or someone else tried to book him. We did it with no hesitation. We paid $2,500 to rent out the biggest club in Brevard County and spent another couple thousand dollars on bottles. In total we spent roughly $15,000 on the event. We divided the cost evenly between the four of us with high hopes of getting our money back plus profit. That was another reason we had come together, to throw big events like that without having to come out of the pocket individually and it lowered the risk.

Since we were new to throwing events with big artists in big clubs, we hired my big dawg T.O. to help orchestrate the night. We had strippers, our own bottles for sale, and we started off charging $50 to get in. I think that's where we went wrong. Our county is a love-hate type of place. Sometimes, people love what you are doing but hate to see you get rich doing it. Even though folks would happily pay $50 to see YFN Lucci in Orlando, they were not interested in giving the same money to us at the door.

If I knew then what I know today, we would have started off with a $20 admission just to pack the building and go up on the price as the night went on. Overall, we had a good crowd. There were a lot of *baddies* and a lot of real *get money* type of dudes from Brevard and 772. YFN Lucci put on an awesome show, and we celebrated all night. We got high, we got drunk, and we had a great time.

Once the night was over, we went back to the hotel to count the money. We made roughly $12,000 back and took a $3,000 loss. We were surprised we took a loss, but we also understood a lot of people didn't come because they felt like they were helping us get rich.

The more exposure we brought to ourselves the more the devil started knocking at our door. Boo was the biggest and youngest hustler from the *800s* at that time and he was just starting to rise. That's when the hate came. Dew had ties with *800 Bound,* but he wasn't all the way solidified as a member. He felt because he committed crimes and went to prison with some of the original *800 Bound* members, Boo and everyone else owed him respect.

We allowed Dew in, and he became a part of *Deaf Row*. There were nights we let Dew sleep in the studio. We all loved Dew but for some reason he hated Boo. Plenty of times they fought then loved each other again like brothers.

<u>2015</u>

August 11, 2015, Dew made up his mind he was going to kill Boo. He showed up at Boo's mother's house and waited for Boo to come home. Once he saw Boo's car hit the street, he immediately started shooting at him. Boo parked the car, calmly got out, and returned fire; hitting Dew in the chest. Dew died that day. I wasn't there. All I remember is that Boo posted on social media, "Somebody better come get Dew. He is in Space Coast Gardens dead."

True enough he was dead. The police eventually came and arrested Boo and charged him with murder. Around the same time, Jae and Ken's house was broken into. The police came to the scene to investigate the break-in and ended up searching the house. Jae's cousin was in possession of stolen identity and devices to commit fraud. The police arrested him, and he snitched on Ken and Jae, who were then indicted on federal charges. That was the end of *Deaf Row Hit Squad*. After two years, Boo beat the murder charge and came home.

# 11

# The Next Decade

By the age of twenty-five, I had a five-year-old daughter, and it had been ten years since the day I *hopped off the porch*; ten years since the day I sold my first drug; and ten years since I had sex for the first time.

I reflected on the first ten years of my music career journey. We still lived in the heart of the hood. I made up my mind I wouldn't leave the hood until I could get my mom out, too. I also made up my mind to be completely done with my baby's mother. She moved on and found a dude she was interested in building with.

Around this time, I met a young, sexy, chocolate female, named Octavia. I met her in the McDonald's drive thru. She was working the window and there was something about her that made me fall for her instantaneously. I knew none of my homies had touched her and she wasn't in every dude's face. She was *put up* and I wanted to make her mine, even though she was dating someone else at the time. I respected her situation, and I continued doing me.

I took other females on dates and posted *all* of them on my Snapchat. I was single so I didn't care. I let every girl I took on a date know that we

♪

were *just* friends, nothing more. Whatever they decided to do after that was their choice, but we would not be classified as more than friends. I was doing me.

I swiped up on Octavia's story and told her, "The only reason why I'm going on these dates with these females is because you *playin'*."

Eventually, I caught her going through a single phase and I took her on a date. We went to City Walk in Orlando. I told her, "It's June 6, 2015. Mark it on your calendar, five years from now, you are going to be mine." We shared our first kiss at the red-light leaving City Walk that night. We built a friendship. She wasn't completely over her ex. They got back together but we stayed in touch.

I decided to take rap more seriously and drop another mixtape. I wanted to focus on myself this time, and not collaborate with any other rappers. Two R & B artists were featured, Detee and Taylor Martin. My goal was to show everyone I can make a classic mixtape without trying to include other rappers. That's how I got my name in the first place. I wanted to go back to my roots and do the things that made me who I am. I released my project titled, *10 Years Later*. I paid DJ DA to host it and I paid for my hit single, "On The Way Up" to get in rotation on the local radio station. I did a radio interview with DJ DA and we promoted the release. He also was the main DJ at the mixtape release party. We worked together so much that I made him my official DJ.

DJ DA was *buzzing* hard; he was always in the club breaking records. I felt like he didn't believe in my project as much as I believed in it. He didn't go over and beyond to break my records in the club or put me on the stage. I felt like I was giving him a title that he wasn't trying to live up to.

When I released the mixtape on all major platforms, I did it without DJ DA hosting it and kept it original. The mixtape was a great body of work, but I didn't follow up with music videos. I didn't even finish passing out the CDs. I dropped that project at the age of twenty-six. Around that time in my life, I realized I couldn't keep spending all my money on my music career.

It was time to create back up plans. I invested $5,500 into a trade and became a licensed barber. I knew I couldn't get away with selling drugs for the rest of my life without getting caught. I kept *grinding* in the *streets* until I got enough money to help my mom move out.

2017

In 2017, we finally moved from Hickory Lane and out of the hood. We spent twenty years on that 800 block. The eviction I received with my baby's mother was now off my credit. I had proof of income through my LLC and my mom had a job.

We both signed the lease, and we moved to Rockledge. This page had to turn for me to move into the next chapter of my life. I was happy for us.

My mom and I became roommates. She didn't bother me, and I didn't bother her. She did her own thing, and I did mine. She made sure I *stayed* with a nice home cooked meal, and she washed my clothes. I'm very appreciative of my mom because without her I would have been *headfirst* into the *streets*. Her acceptance of my lifestyle kept me away from a lot of trouble.

Everything I did in the *streets* I left it in the *streets*. We still had access to our old house in the hood, so I *trapped* out of there while living in the next city over. I *served* weed to all the big-time dope boys in my area. One older dude named G used to pull up on me and spend hundreds of dollars at a time. We *chopped it up* more and more every time he pulled up on me. One day he told me, "Lil' bra, I'm really up. I got so much money put up I don't even touch it."

My response was, "I have a master plan. If you're down to invest into my brain we can split the business 50/50."

He agreed. He also recommended we should sit down with a lawyer first. I already had a business attorney who handled all my business filings. I scheduled an appointment for us to meet with my lawyer and we started the process. Before we started going *hard* into the business, I warned him that the devil will plot to attack us when he sees us on a road toward success. I told him to keep the business between us so we can work in *silence.* I didn't tell anyone about our business move and kept it private.

When we sat down with my lawyer and discussed percentages, we both agreed he was 100% muscle, and I was 100% brain. We split the business 50/50 because we knew one was just as powerful as the other and the business would not be able to operate without both. We came up with the name *CFN International*, signed the paper-work, and became business partners.

My last experience working with a group of *homeboys* didn't end the way I had anticipated. They gave up on *our* vision once things started going bad. Then again, I felt like I may have forced my vision on them. It wasn't something they were really interested in. I knew everyone couldn't see my vision, so I didn't *fall out* with them, we stayed in touch.

I learned a lot of skills when I managed the studio we created, *Deaf Row.* I designed the whole layout, made sure the bills were paid, oversaw the finances, and developed a high-quality studio. I was confident that if I did it before, I could do it again, even better.

I did more research and found the best equipment to buy and techniques to soundproof the room. Also, I had my barber's license, and I knew everything required to open a barbershop. I told G, we can do both under the same roof. Nobody we knew of had a barbershop and a recording studio under the same roof. We had the money and brains to do it.

It just so happened that his aunt and uncle were managing a strip plaza, and they had spaces for lease. We saw the perfect space for the vision I had in mind. The rooms were already laid out how we needed them to be. There was only a little carpentry work that needed to be done. Another 'coincidence,' G's uncle did carpentry work. I told him, "God is really on our side with all of this, everything is lining up perfect and it's out of our control." We signed our lease and got to work immediately. We had meetings with the city of Cocoa to make sure all the licensing was correct, and they told us everything the building needed to have in order to open. We knocked out all the hard work. Within ten months of silent *grinding,* we were ready to publicly announce our business venture together.

Even more coincidentally, G and I share the same birthday. We went to Miami for the weekend before our birthday. G had a *crib* down there and it was spring break. After all the hard work we put in, we were ready to hang out. We quickly grew a brotherly bond. He admired how I carried myself and how I stood on business. I appreciated him for believing in me. When our birthday came around, I posted a picture of us *vibin'* on South Beach. I wished the both of us a happy birthday and I introduced everyone to our new business venture. That's when the devil started knocking on the front door, again.

## 12
# Came From Nothing

G invested everything we needed to get the carpentry work done. We had new floors, new baseboards, and freshly painted walls. We sound proofed the recording room and engineering room with installation and acoustic treatment. The barbershop was adorned with marble counters, three individual workstations, new leather furniture, and a big 75-inch flat screen television for the lobby.

We drove to Sam Ash in Orlando, Florida to get all the studio equipment. G bought everything we needed except for the computer. I told him I had an Apple MacBook Pro laptop to use and that saved him a few thousand dollars. Once we hooked everything up and got it running correctly, I sat down with a graphic designer and came up with our logo. We revised it a few times until we got it exactly how I liked it. I showed it to G, and he was amazed. He paid for the logo design, and he paid for three big decal stickers. I envisioned the logo being placed on our wooden floor just like the center of a basketball court. That's exactly how we did it and we also put the logo on the walls. Everything turned out great and was going as planned. G invested roughly twenty thousand dollars for everything up to this point.

I came up with a plan to get us the most exposure possible to make our debut. I knew YNW Melly before the fame and we frequently stayed in contact with each other. YNW Melly and JGreen were like my lil brothers. We didn't hang around each other because I was a lot older, but we had great respect for one another. JGreen used to come to my KMAFT events and perform. The first time he came he performed for free, that's the type of relationship we had. The other times, I paid him five hundred dollars and he rocked the crowd for me. YNW Melly was scheduled to come *show me love* and perform but he ended up getting locked up.

While he was doing his juvenile bid, we messaged each other on social media. I told him when he got out, we were going to get some money together and I truly believed he would become a superstar. His manager, 100K Track, ended up signing him while he was still incarcerated. Once he was released from jail, TMak booked him for a show instantly. TMak is a legendary club promoter in Brevard County. He often brought a lot of big-name artists to the city. My plan to help manage YNW Melly was out the window and I was too slow on booking him for a show. So, the only option I had left was to pay him for a feature.

I told G about YNW Melly and how he was becoming this huge rap artist. I came up with the idea to book another artist by the name of JayDaYoungan for a show and to feature on a song. On that same song, we would pay YNW Melly to do a hook and a verse on it. JayDaYoungan was just starting to get a *buzz* also, and I saw the potential in him. We were one of the first people to book him for a show in Florida. YNW Melly wanted $2,500 for the feature. JayDaYoungan wanted $5,000 for the show and $2,500 for the feature. The club owner wanted $1,500 to book the club for the night. We also paid Kodak Black's 'first love' Cali Paradise $1,000 to host the event. With G being the muscle and me being the brain, G paid for everything.

YNW Melly's manager hit me up and said they were going to come through the club and show JayDaYoungan some love in VIP. I got excited because I knew that would bring extra hype to our event. After talking it over with G we decided to make a social media post letting everyone know that YNW Melly would be in VIP at JayDaYoungan's show. As soon as I made the post, YNW Melly's manager called me and said Melly needs $1,000 or he won't come to the event, and he wouldn't want to do the feature anymore. They felt as if we were getting free promotion from Melly's face since no one was supposed to know he was coming. G was already deeply invested so I paid YNW Melly $1,000 myself.

The event did good, there was a decent-sized crowd, but we didn't make back all the money we invested into the event. G spent roughly $12,000 and I spent $1,000. We made approximately $7,500 back from ticket sales and the money at the door. We still had to pay JayDaYoungan $2,500 for the feature.

The event ended with a shootout, and everyone scattered to their cars. That didn't stop anything. JayDaYoungan and YNW Melly came to the studio after the club. G started feeling like he was wasting a lot of money and had second thoughts. The whole time I saw the potential and greatness in such a big collaboration. Producers iPound and Ronnie Doe from South Florida came to the studio. Shube was the engineer that night and this became our first official studio session.

I had a Canon camera I bought for $2,500. I had gotten tired of paying local camera men $150 just to get footage for me at my events. Most of the time they acted like they were too busy to record. So, I recorded everything from this event myself.

I introduced YNW Melly to JayDaYoungan and they made a *hot* song together titled, "We Want Smoke" and I was the executive producer. There were so many people in the studio that night. A lot of fans followed us over to the studio. We drunk, smoked, and had a good time. We didn't leave the studio until five in the morning. The next day, I woke up to G having second thoughts about our business deal. He didn't understand what took place that night. He was more concerned about the money we lost.

A few days passed and my friends Boo and Ken wanted to book studio time. G assumed I fell out with my friends once we started doing business together and he didn't like them. He didn't want them to record in our studio. They were paying customers, in fact our first paying customers, and he wanted me to make them leave.

We got into an argument, and I told him the *streets* said he was working with the police. At the time I thought it was only a rumor, but I didn't care because I wasn't doing any *dirt* with him. We were involved in a legit business. When he tried to get me involved in his operation, I turned it down. I told him we were only business partners, and I don't mix legit business with the *streets*. He decided since he invested a lot of money into the business he would change the percentages. We came into the initial business agreement as 50/50 partners. He was the muscle, and I was the brain. Now, he wanted to include his brother, who knew nothing about the business. G proposed he would own 50 percent of the business and his brother and I would split the other 50 percent, 25/25.

Obviously, that led to a big disagreement, and I decided to no longer do business with him.

Just like I said in the beginning, the devil will come, and he came. My million-dollar business plan ended before it even started. G felt like since everything was up and running, he didn't need me anymore. He had the barbershop, and he had the studio. I guess he figured he could hire barbers and engineers to run the spot and my job in the business was no longer needed. What he didn't know was he couldn't do it without me because it was my vision.

I went to the Dodge dealership and left the lot in a brand-new Dodge Challenger. I pulled up on him at the studio and told him to come outside. I wanted to look him in the face while I gave him his key to the building back. He didn't expect me to pull up in a new car. He thought I was broke and that I needed him. In reality, he needed me, and I knew that. I gave him his key and took everything that belonged to me including my MacBook Pro and camera. I let him have my whole business plan and wished him good luck.

# 13
# Realer Than Most

<u>End of 2018 – 2019</u>

Before I called it quits with G I held a meeting with my bros. Ken, Jae, Boo, and I met at the restaurant, Applebee's, to discuss everything that went down. They told me how none of this would have happened if they supported my vision and they were behind any decision I made dealing with G.

It was now the end of 2018 going into 2019. Around this time, I worked for a company in Orlando building boats. I was out of the *streets*, but I still did a little *hustling* on the side here and there for extra money. I worked 50 plus hours a week. I woke up at 4 o' clock in the morning every day for work.

Octavia and I became closer friends. It got to the point that she would stay the night with me every night. Her boyfriend finally slipped up and let me get her. Once we started *vibin'* more, I made it my business to show her I was the realest dude she ever met. Every weekend we hung out whether it was going out to eat, to the movies, or somewhere else, it was always a night of fun. I was no longer interested in *messing* with any other female. I had to make her mine. My life was simple.

I would work, go to the studio, and chill with my family.

I decided to start working on another mixtape and really put my time, quality, and dedication into the project. I had to make this tape the best tape of my career. I wanted to make sure I had a feature from all my bros on it. I recorded at one of the best studios in Central Florida. We traveled to Altamonte Springs to 212 Recording Studio frequently. That's where I recorded my whole project. It got to the point where all of my homies started going there to record their music. I wanted the quality to be the best I ever released, so I paid top dollar for them to record, mix, and master all of my tracks.

Ken and Jae were out on federal bond awaiting sentencing and we wanted to get as much work done as possible. January 24, 2019, I was going through my camera roll and looking at all the footage I recorded. I just so happened to scroll across footage from the night YNW Melly and JayDaYoungan were in the studio. A voice in my head told me to upload the video on to my YouTube channel and see what happens. So, I did it and I named it "YNW Melly & JayDaYoungan unreleased full video". Unexpectedly, the video gained five to ten thousand views a day.

I quickly made a phone call to the producers Ronnie Doe and iPound. I told them to check out my YouTube channel. They were surprised and super excited because this was the most attention their beats ever got. I told them I had the laptop we recorded the session on, and I would try to pull it up so we could work on releasing it. For some odd reason, I could not find the files at the time, and I almost gave up.

A few weeks later, February 13, 2019, YNW Melly was arrested and charged with double homicide. His two best friends, YNW Sakchaser and YNW Juvy were murdered. The police accused YNW Melly of killing his two friends and staging a drive by attack. Their other friend, YNW Bortlen, drove the two to the hospital where they were pronounced dead. My video went from ten thousand views a day to over twenty thousand views a day. YNW Melly was trending worldwide. No one could believe something like that really happened.

After seeing my video go viral, I made one more attempt to find the studio session files. It was a miracle; I found them and I had every vocal YNW Melly ever recorded at the studio that night. I quickly called the producers and told them I found the session and I wanted to buy exclusive rights to the beat. They charged me $400 and sent over the contract. I called the head engineer at 212 Recording Studio and told JP about the single and that I needed the song mixed and mastered to perfection as soon as possible. I emailed him the studio session files and the instrumental tracked out with every instrument on its own track. He charged me $200 for the mix and master. I spent another $250 for the artwork needed for the single cover.

Once I got everything back, I went to my distribution website and uploaded it. I scheduled it to be released on my birthday weekend. After I submitted it for distribution, the streaming platforms denied it. They said I needed a contract stating I own rights to the song and YNW Melly's manager 100K Track had to give it to me. I called him day after day. I left messages on his phone, in his direct messenger on social media, and sent multiple emails. I never got a response until I threatened to take legal action. I told him I would get my lawyer involved if he didn't send over the contract because I have been asking for this contract for the past year. I previously paid him through a wire transfer and had proof of doing business, so he had no choice but to send it over. Once I received it, I quickly submitted it. Everything was approved and YNW Melly featuring JaydaYoungan, "We Want Smoke" was set to be released March 29, 2019. That was the weekend after my birthday, so it was a double celebration.

I told Jae, Ken, and Boo about the song and explained how I got everything cleared. All I needed was a budget for promotion and the rest was history. The week before my birthday Jae and I went *on a mission* together and I *hit a lick* for a large amount of money. Octavia and I decided to go to New Orleans for a popular hair convention. She is originally from New Orleans, so I had a chance to meet a lot of her family members, and we hung out *good.* We ate at every restaurant we wanted. We hung out on Bourbon Street all night. We got drunk, went to the casino, and lost a few hundred dollars.

My song was released on all major platforms that Friday on the 29th, and generated 15,000 streams in one day on Apple Music. I knew I had a hit. This was the first song I ever executively produced with two platinum selling artists. I paid for flyers and posters to be printed, and I brought them to New Orleans with us. Octavia wanted to become a full-time hair stylist, and I was into learning more about barbering, so the hair convention was a perfect date for us. There were thousands of people in and out of the event center and a few celebrities were there. I met the rap artist and actor Bow Wow for the first time. I also met 360 Jeezy, one of the barbers I used to watch on YouTube a lot. Octavia participated in the hair competition, and she did great.

We were having a great time until we woke up that Sunday morning. We were in our hotel room when I scrolled on Instagram and saw that Nipsey Hussle was shot and fighting for his life. They pronounced him dead later that day and it hurt me badly. Out of all the rappers in the game I admired Nipsey Hustle. I didn't know a lot of his music, but I will always admire his hustler's ambition. He reminded me so much of myself when it came to doing everything independently. We shared some of the same traits and stood on a lot of the same principles. I was mad he was taken away so soon and I never got a chance to meet him. That stayed on my mind for the rest of the trip. I felt like I had to keep the marathon going and remain one of the real ones no matter what.

Our trip ended and I went home to more drama. G was on social media telling everyone I'm a snake, I'm broke, and I ran off with his song. In reality, I felt like it was an even trade. I literally gave him my million-dollar plan and told him to keep it. In exchange, I took everything that belonged to me, which was my laptop. Just so happened, the studio files were still on there. Without my brain, there wouldn't be a studio, barbershop, or song. I took what was rightfully mine. He thought he could run the business without me. He hired barbers to come in to cut hair. He hired engineers to run the studio. The whole city knew it was my plan that he stole, so his support was limited. The business ended up going downhill. The engineer he hired was young and a little naive when it came to the *streets*. So, he manipulated him to do business with him. The same business I turned down the young engineer agreed to because he needed the money. I tried to warn the engineer that G was a shady person and if he did me *dirty*, he would be no different. He didn't listen to me and proceeded to do business with him.

That summer was lit for the bros and I. We made so much money, however it all came to a halt fast. Jae and Ken had to turn themselves in to serve their federal prison bid. Boo and I tried to keep things in motion by continuing to get money like before, but it wasn't the same. It seemed like everything stopped working once they got locked up. I took it as a sign and got another job. Octavia and I moved into our first apartment together and became a couple. We lived in a luxury apartment in a gated community.

I had enough money saved up to put into my mixtape. I named this tape, "Realer Than Most". I featured all my bros and I included the song I executively produced with YNW Melly and JayDaYoungan as a bonus track. Tmak booked my album release party at a strip club in Cocoa Beach. The homies from the block came out to support me on stage. It was a fun night, and I received great feedback from my mixtape.

Less than a week after my mixtape dropped Boo was arrested for *running* the police. I felt like I was out here by myself. I also felt like it was a sign from God. I had gotten word from *the inside* that I was being targeted by the Feds. I stopped everything I thought I was doing illegally and tried to survive on a 9 to 5 wage. Even though my biological dad and I haven't always had a good relationship, somehow, he always seemed to help me find a job when I needed one. He put in a word for me, and I started working for a company that builds electronic pieces for airplanes. It was an okay paying job. It was just enough to pay my bills, so I didn't complain.

My mixtape ended up doing over 1 million streams and became the biggest mixtape of my career, as I predicted. My passion to become a rapper wasn't the same though. I felt like everyone who I wanted to bring with me was locked up and I didn't want to do it alone. I shot a video tribute to all my homies who were locked up, featuring R&B singer Taylor Martin on the hook and Jae on the second verse before he got locked up. My big bro Diddy was in the *pen* serving a 10-year bid. Jae and Ken were locked in the Feds serving their bid. Boo was locked in the county jail with no bond. I just wanted to lay low while I enjoyed my girl and my family.

<u>2020</u>

I got word that G was busted by the Feds. He was caught doing business with a federal informant. Instead of taking his charges and doing his time, he made it seem like the young engineer was the one doing all the dirt. He snitched on lil homie and both of them were indicted by the Feds. I dodged a major bullet because a lot of people told me he was the police, but I had given him the benefit of the doubt because we were doing legit business. All I could think about were all the times he tried to influence me to sell drugs with him. I was smart enough to *not* get involved and it saved me. God don't like ugly. He tried to make it seem like I was a snake and the whole time it was him. I literally dodged a federal indictment.

I ended up getting laid off from my job due to a cut back. I decided to take barbering more seriously. I didn't really know how to cut hair, and I didn't want to mess up anybody's head who I knew personally, so I started working in a mostly Caucasian based barbershop. I wanted to learn how to cut their hair first because if I messed up at least I didn't know them, and they paid more.

Spring of 2020, my 30th birthday, was approaching. I wanted to go out of town to celebrate with my girl, but the world had other plans. The coronavirus hit the United States hard and caused a countrywide shut down. I couldn't work at the barbershop anymore; they forced us to close, and we were stuck inside the house. It was a horrible way to spend my 30th birthday. I had to make the best of it, so I threw a party at the studio and invited some of the homies to come through. We made music for five hours straight. We had food, liquor, and weed. It was a nice *vibe*.

During the shutdown, the government sent out stimulus checks and other benefits to help us survive. Eventually, that money ran out and I was down to my last thousand dollars on my credit card. When Octavia cooked us dinner, she'd make a fruit smoothie for dessert. It was one of the best smoothies I ever tasted. It was perfectly blended and all natural. We were studying Doctor Sebi and his cure for colds and viruses. That's when we learned about seamoss and the natural health benefits this sea vegetable is packed with. As we looked more into it, we learned it is packed with 92 nutrients and minerals. Once it is cleaned and soaked, it can be blended with alkaline water and turned into a gel. A tablespoon a day has been said to help prevent viruses, act as a natural energy booster, help decrease inflammation and help improve the digestive system. It has been called an all-around super food.

As we continued to research, I came up with a bright idea. I told Octavia, "Instead of putting liquor in the smoothies, how about we put seamoss in them and sell them for $10?"

During the peak of the pandemic the world needed a product like this. She agreed that it was a great idea, so we went *all in.* I invested my last $1,000 into creating a new business, Superior Soul Supplements. The startup cost wasn't expensive at all because seamoss is inexpensive compared to the profit margin. We bought a pound of it and had it shipped to us. I cleaned it, soaked it, and turned it into a gel. Octavia made the smoothies, and we put a tablespoon of seamoss into each one. We couldn't taste the seamoss at all, and the smoothie was delicious. That's when I knew we were on to something. We found a print company and paid them to design our logo, flyer, and stickers for the bottles. All of that was roughly $500 in all. We paid $100 for our photoshoot. $170 for 150 bottles and the rest we spent on fruit. We announced our new business in the most professional way possible. Everything was legit from the flyers to the product. Everyone wanted to try them. We had 4 different flavors: Mango Passion, Tropical Paradise, Detox, and Berry Sensation. We ended up selling over 700 smoothies in our first couple months of business. Yep, that's right $10 times 700. We made $7,000 dollars and Superior Soul Supplements was in demand.

After being around each other for two years straight, we realized we were really soulmates and both agreed we were ready to bring a kid into the world. We tried and tried and tried again until one day our dreams came true. Octavia was pregnant. *What else was there to do during a nationwide shut down?* (Laughing my butt off.) We knew we would be the perfect parents, no matter the circumstances of the world. Both of us were already very ambitious entrepreneurs and we were best friends.

As we were approaching the final months of our lease, I recommended we start our family in Atlanta, Georgia. I felt like my time in Brevard County had expired. All of my bros were locked up and there wasn't anything for us to look forward to there. We knew we could pursue our careers in the beauty industry, in the lucrative city of Atlanta. We also knew if we sold 700 smoothies in Brevard County we could sell way more in Atlanta. We called around to search for apartments in Atlanta until we found the one we felt was a good fit for us. The world was still in a pandemic, so we had to do a virtual tour of the apartment. We decided on a one-bedroom / one-bathroom and we signed the lease online. June 2020, we packed up our things and headed to Atlanta with a baby on the way.

# 14
# Moved Away To Make A Way

I never liked being comfortable, I love being challenged. Once things become easy for me, I tend to add more to my plate. We didn't have a lot of money saved up. I had roughly $12,000 dollars to my name in total. We had no jobs secured and Octavia was pregnant for the first time during the peak of covid. We moved away from our family and chose a fresh start in a new environment.

I wrote letters and set up visits to stay in touch with my bros. I told them by the time they came home I would no longer be living in Brevard County. They probably didn't take me seriously; people always tend to underestimate me.

Summer of 2020

On the Southside of Atlanta, Jonesboro, Georgia was the city we would call home. We hired movers to unload the moving truck, and we finished unpacking everything. My oldest daughter Zari came with us for her summer break.

One day we stopped by a local restaurant to grab something to eat. Right next to the restaurant was a barbershop. I walked in and introduced myself to the owner. His name was Vic. Vic was an older dude; we had similarities from day one. We were both from Florida, and we *packed* a lot of corporate and street knowledge. I told him I had my license to cut hair in Florida, but I wasn't comfortable cutting yet. In fact, I didn't know how to cut African American hair at all, and only had three months of experience cutting Caucasian hair before the world shutdown. He told me he was willing to work with me if I was willing to take it seriously. He introduced me to his partner Ty. Ty was really cool from the beginning. She let me shadow her and gave me a few pointers.

I told Vic I only wanted to cut the heads I felt comfortable cutting until I mastered the skills needed because I didn't want to make a bad name for his shop. I wanted to perfect basic cuts first. I wanted to learn how to do an all even cut then start working on fading. I did start cutting hair in the barbershop, but it came to an end quickly. The shop didn't have any air conditioning, and it was blazing hot outside. On top of that, Vic would catch an attitude with me when I chose not to cut certain clients. I told him thanks for the opportunity and that I appreciated everything, but I could no longer work in his shop.

After leaving Vic's barbershop I called around looking for other barbering opportunities. After a few calls, I landed a new job opportunity at a different shop. I liked the environment, it was super clean, and everyone seemed to be in good spirits. This shop had more barbers than the last shop. They were all older than me, around the age of 50. Mr. Monte was the owner. He ran his shop differently. It was mostly a walk-in barbershop, with an online booking system. I told him I had a FL license, but I was inexperienced when it came to barbering. I let him know I was a fast learner, and I was dedicated to the process. He gave me an opportunity to cut hair in his shop. I watched the other barbers' techniques, and some of them came over to correct me when they saw me messing up. I told Mr. Monte the same thing I told Vic, I only want to cut the heads I'm comfortable with until I master more skills. I don't want to make a bad reputation for your barbershop.

I'm not going to lie; I missed out on a lot of money by picking and choosing my cuts. I had the other barbers in the shop feeling *some type of way*. They didn't like the fact that I chose the *easy* walk-ins and passed up the clients who needed to be faded. It was hard to build a clientele without being confident in my cuts. I wasn't making enough money to pay my bills, and my funds were running low. I told Mr. Monte about my situation and that I appreciated the opportunity, but I needed to find a job with steady income.

That's when I came up with my next plan. I knew if I did what it took to raise my credit score to 700 and I had proof of income then I could get anything I wanted. I went on a job search. I walked into a few warehouses. I knew warehouse jobs were in demand and the pay was good enough to get the bills paid. I eventually left one of the warehouses with a job opportunity. I became a certified forklift driver making $17 an hour. I worked the 3rd shift overnight, and Octavia found a work from home job and continued doing hair on the side. My primary goal was to pay all my main bills and consolidate my credit card debt. After a few months of working, I had my credit cards consolidated into one monthly payment.

Toward the end of 2020, Jae and Ken were both released from the Feds. They served a few months in and the rest of their sentence out on probation. When they came home it was a different *vibe*. Not to brag on what I did or to even say I did a lot, but I kept all the bros' names alive their whole bid. I ran Jae's social media accounts and kept him in the eyes of the people. I made sure I looked out for their kids even though I was struggling to pay my own bills. I bought gifts for their kids' birthdays, and I stayed in touch with their babies' mothers in case they needed anything. I uplifted them their whole bid. We all agreed, we would get back to where we left off once everyone was free. It seemed as if they weren't happy I had made it out and wanted better for myself. They never congratulated me, or said I'm proud of you, or anything in that nature.

Instead, they got out and felt like they had a point to prove. They hung out with dudes who didn't ride for them while they were locked up. They randomly bought expensive jewelry, clothes, and shoes. All that, to let everyone know they didn't miss a beat and they're back. I felt played so I started making indirect posts on my social media expressing my feelings. I never mentioned any names but anyone who knew the situation knew who I was talking about. My exact words were, "If I considered someone my brother, I wouldn't leave him out." Then Jae *hit me up* trying to put me *on game*. By that time, it was too late. I made the investment, and I took a loss. My daughter's birthday and Christmas were approaching, and I was broke. I told Jae his route wasn't meant to become my route; I tried it, and I lost. I proceeded to tell him I had a lot of good things in motion to get us legit money. I had my *Realer Than Most* clothing line, selling hundreds of hoodies; and Superior Soul Supplements, selling thousands of smoothies. Also, I was getting better at cutting hair and I had millions of streams from my music. I asked Jae, "Are you down to get money with my plan like I was down for your plan?"

He told me he had my back, but his actions spoke differently. I had a weird feeling that Jae and Ken wanted me to continue risking my life, on their plan. But I knew if we worked together on my plan, nobody would have to risk their life again. They knew I was the last one left in our group who had a clean record, and I wasn't going to jeopardize my freedom anymore. Once I saw they didn't believe in my vision, I fell completely back from them.

Boo eventually got out of the county jail and into a lot of beef with other gangs around town. I saw God separating me from them right before my eyes. He didn't allow them to help me because He knew I would have given them a lot of praise when I was supposed to be praising the Lord. Once I saw all the signs, I realized I had to experience the next part of my journey without them.

Octavia and I went to the ultrasound facility and found out we were having a baby girl. I was calling our baby Junior the whole time just to find out I'm a full-blown girl dad. At first, I was upset but then I got over it. I knew I had to become a better man for my little girls. We didn't have a baby shower due to covid, so our family and friends sent us baby gifts through the mail. On February 26, 2021, my second child Taliyah Sanaa Waller was born at Northside Hospital in Atlanta, Georgia. Octavia was overdue and Taliyah did not want to come out, so the doctor performed a C-section. Other than that, we had a healthy covid baby. We had no family to help us during this process because the hospital didn't allow any visitors.

My mom and Zari came to see her after we were released from the hospital. A couple of months later, Octavia and I caught the covid virus. I lost my senses of smell and taste. My respiratory system was a little off and I was congested but I made it through. Octavia on the other hand was admitted into the hospital and had to stay there for five days because her oxygen levels were low. I was home alone with our newborn baby. Thank God, it didn't affect her, and Octavia overcame the virus.

Our first year living in Atlanta was difficult but we got through it together. Both of our cars were broken into at our apartment complex, and we heard gun shots every other week. We thought we picked the right location, but it reminded us of our hometown of Cocoa, FL. I eventually got my credit score up to 730 and I had proof of income. I qualified for some personal loans and credit cards totaling up to $30,000. Now that the baby was born, and we had my oldest daughter visiting a lot, we needed more space. I used $10,000 of the money to get us into a new home. I paid the first month, last month, and the security deposit in order to move in. We broke our lease with the apartment and moved into a newly built two-story house on the outskirts of Atlanta. I made sure we were in a great environment and Octavia could work from home in peace.

I also invested in some high-quality studio equipment with hopes of finding a location to establish and run a studio. Everywhere I went they denied opening a studio. They didn't want loud music affecting other businesses.

<u>2022</u>

After working at the warehouse for a year and a few months, I walked out January 22, 2022. They hired me to be a forklift driver, but the supervisor kept making me do other tasks outside of my job description. I told myself if she asked me to do someone else's job again, I was walking out. She asked me that morning and that's exactly what I did. That was the last day working there for me.

I decided I was going to give barbering my all this time. I went back to Mr. Monte and told him my situation. He figured since we didn't end on bad terms and I sounded a lot more dedicated he would give me another try. That's all I needed, and I started perfecting my craft. During my first full year of cutting hair, my skills advanced tremendously, and I cleared over $60,000.

Since it was so hard to find a standalone spot for a studio, I gave in and hired some carpenters to build a studio in my garage. My cousin Surhonda lived a few miles away and she wanted to lend a helping hand. She cleaned up as the carpenters finished working, laid the floor down in the garage, and bought some plug-ins for my recording software. I really appreciate her because she did all of that without me asking. She saw my vision and wanted to help bring it to life.

I eventually linked up with Vic again. He had a new business venture, and he was leasing an old bank on the Southside. He had barber and stylist suites for rent, and a lot of open space. I told him about the equipment I had and how I built everything in my house because I couldn't find space. Coincidentally, he had an empty room which looked like a recording studio already there. It just needed some touching up and the equipment. We decided to go into business together even though we had differences regarding barbering. We felt we could be beneficial to one another, and it would be a good look to run the studio out of there. I moved all my equipment there and my cousin Surhonda was down to help bring it to life once again. We worked hard to get everything up and running just for the whole building to get closed down in one day. The studio was perfect. The set-up was nice and neat thanks to big cuz's carpentry work.

## 2023

January 24, 2023, was our first studio session. An up-and-coming local artist by the name of Anti Da Menace was the first to book our studio. I was plugged in with A&R Rique, we are both from Cocoa and admired each other's work. He plugged me in with Anti Da Menace and we let him throw his listening party at our studio for free in exchange for some exposure. We didn't know he would bring so many people. Everyone rolled up their own weed, smoked, and had a good time. Everything was great until the fire alarm went off. Vic wasn't there, he left the engineer and I to run the night ourselves. I called him panicking, trying to figure out how to turn the alarm off. He was far away and couldn't come to turn it off. We tried to do it over the phone, but it didn't work. I made everyone leave the studio before the fire marshal pulled up. When they arrived, the whole building was filled with smoke. We cleaned up the studio in time but couldn't rid the air of the smoke. The fire marshal silenced the alarm and told us to have a great night.

The next morning Vic called me crying and said he lost the building. I felt bad but I also knew it wasn't solely my fault. We were partners and that was our first session. We both should have been there to ensure everything went smoothly. The situation was out of my control once the alarm went off. Other than that, there were no problems. The City of Morrow said that was the final strike. Vic had other run-ins with the city due to previous violations, and our incident forced them to close the establishment down. I packed all my equipment up and moved everything back to my house. I set up my studio and began to record new music at home.

Once Mr. Monte saw my improvement in the barbershop, I thought he would be proud of me. Instead, he became a big hater. I was an independent contractor, which means I paid booth rent and worked for myself. He had it in his mind that I worked for him. He didn't want me to book my clients' appointments. He wanted to control what time I came in and what time I left. I was working six days a week in his shop, and it still wasn't enough for him. One day he wanted me to open the shop, but I couldn't because I was watching my daughter. I still ended up being the first one there and opened the shop. One of the other barbers said he would open, but he didn't come in until one o'clock in the afternoon. For some reason, Mr. Monte wanted to have a meeting with both of us to explain to him why his shop wasn't open on time. I told him the night before I wouldn't be able to do it, but he insisted on having a meeting with both of us. My response was, "When everything fails, if no one else is available, then it's the owner's responsibility to make sure the shop is open." He got mad at me for standing up for myself and told me to get out of his shop and I did. May 2023, I built a barbershop in my home and started cutting there.

<u>2024</u>

By 2024, I was completely independent. I also enrolled in school to become an HVAC Technician. I've even met a few celebrities our first few years living in Georgia. I met Gucci Mane; Kandi from the group Xscape; comedian Desi Banks; rap artists Latto, 2 Chainz, and Yung Joc; and Shaquille O'Neal.

Out of all the celebrities I met I would say Shaq is the coolest. He's down-to-earth and the fun spirit type. We actually partied together at his daughter Taahirah's private party.

After Shaq, I would say Latto and 2 Chainz seemed very humble. We were invited into Latto's private launch party for Rihanna's lingerie line, *Savage X Fenty*, in Lenox Mall. She took pictures with my whole family, and she was all smiles. I hung out with 2 Chainz and his family on the Southside at his restaurant Escobar South. He was very humble; we chopped it up and I showed him my music stats. He was so impressed that he told me to *link* with his right-hand man. I didn't reach out to him because I never got a chance to let him know it was deeper than rap. He thought I was looking for a record deal, but I wanted him to know I am business minded and similar to him.

I hung out with Gucci Mane all day at his video shoot in Zone 6, East Atlanta. I introduced myself at the end of the shoot, as he was leaving. I tried to give him a flyer sharing all of my businesses as he was rolling up the window in his Phantom. I stuck my hand in the window and he told me to get that mess out of his car and pulled off. I definitely would say that was the worst experience I had meeting a celebrity. I get it, he probably is approached a lot by random people trying to get record deals. That wasn't my intention. My flyer had my four businesses on it. I just wanted him to know I was a young up and coming CEO, just like him. Eventually, we will meet again, and I will tell him this story.

I hung out with Desi Banks at a club event with my lil bro Jamel Dean, the cornerback for the Tampa Bay Buccaneers. Dean and I are from the same city. We have always supported each other so he invited me out to hang with him and his celebrity friends. Desi Banks was cool, we chopped it up for a second and enjoyed the rest of the night.

I briefly met Kandi at her brunch spot. She was down-to-earth, also. I asked her to please take a picture with my daughter Zari and she did.

While living in Atlanta, over the years, I can count on one hand the times I went to an actual club. I've been focusing on getting my household in order and securing my bag.

# 15
# Forgive All; Forget Nothing

After everything I've been through, I realized in order for me to reach the next level in life, I must forgive.

My biological father - I forgive him for not being a major part of my life. Every time we talked, he had an excuse to explain why he wasn't there. He was my grandmother's only child. He grew up very spoiled and he always assumed the world revolved around him. I forgive him for not having a relationship with me or his grandkids. I forgive him for not being a positive role model in my life. He tried to convince me that once I have kids of my own and start dealing with the *baby mama drama*, I would understand. Yes, indeed I had my share of *baby mama drama*, but I didn't let that stop me from having a relationship with my own kids. I know it hurt my dad to hear his son call another man father, but it was only because he gave up on having a relationship with me. Still to this day he doesn't call to see if I'm alive or okay. I will never understand a parent going days, weeks, months, and years without checking on their children. I still forgive him. No, I won't be the bigger person and try to have a relationship with him. No, I won't make it my business to call and check up on him, but I forgive him. I pray one day he will realize the important things in life and learn to take accountability for his actions.

To my childhood friends - I forgive all of you. I know it was hard to believe in someone else's dream while still trying to find yourself. I know it was difficult to see my vision and the possibility of everything coming true. We came from a harsh environment equivalent to crabs in a bucket. I feel like the love I had for my friends was unmatched. I feel like my friends were always in competition with me and tried to prove they were better than me. All I ever wanted to do was see us all become successful. What was mine was theirs but what was theirs wasn't mine. Our friendship may never be the same again, but I don't hold any grudges.

Jae, Ken, and Boo - I looked at them like brothers. I wanted them to get the recognition they deserved for playing a major part in my life. I featured them on my album and decided to let the world hear their voices. We could have been millionaires a long time ago. They didn't see my vision. They didn't want to go all in with me, but I forgive them. The love I showed them made them feel like I needed them in order to succeed. They had other friends they expressed their loyalty to, and they left me to fend for myself, but I forgive them. We haven't sat down to talk about our differences, and I don't plan on doing so. I know for a fact I was a great friend, and I will not be the bigger person to reach out this time. Some people's pride is too big to say, "I'm sorry," and I'm fine with that. Obviously, we were not meant to be as tight as I thought.

To my first baby's mother - I forgive her. I forgive her for not believing in me. I forgive her for not being patient. I forgive her for placing me on child support and getting the government in our business. Year after year she would always tell me I do the bare minimum for our child. I bought the majority of my child's expensive possessions. All the time I invested to teach my daughter as a toddler is one of the main reasons she is an 'A' honor roll student in advanced classes. I told my baby's mother eventually our child will grow up and understand for herself that I was always there. Eventually, the harsh things she said about me will no longer be believable. I forgive her for all the internal pain she caused me. It really hurt me because she promised to never be a bitter baby's mother who would put me on child support. My dad's words always played in the back of my head, and I promised myself, *I will never give up on loving my child.* I forgive her and I'm thankful for how things played out between us. She gave me the opportunity to meet the love of my life.

Last but not least, I forgive myself. I forgive myself for always putting me last. I always showed others more love than I showed myself. I always tried to be *that* friend who I wanted others to be to me. I was always the one motivating others when I really needed some motivation myself. I was always giving others all of my energy when I really needed it for myself to move up to the next level. I feel like I abandoned myself a lot throughout my career just to help others start theirs. I was looking for myself inside of others and that's where I went wrong. I expected my friends to have the same love for me that I had for them. I expected them to look out for me the same way I looked out for them. Nobody told me to stick my neck out and help them. I chose to ride for them while locked up. I chose to show up to court dates when nobody else did. I chose to set up visitations and help boost their spirits. Everything I did I chose to do because I felt it was the right thing to do. Nobody owed me their loyalty in return. Nobody had to give me the same energy I gave them. I forgive myself for going too hard for people who never really cared about me. I forgive myself for not going as hard as I could in my career.

Yes, *I was slept on,* by many people. It hurt me the most when I realized I slept on myself. I promise to dedicate these upcoming years to bettering myself. I deserve to put myself first. I deserve to care about me more than I care about others. I can't save anybody until I save myself. All the good deeds I did for my friends and family went unnoticed. People felt like they didn't have to show me their appreciation. They felt like everything I did for them was the bare minimum.

I always knew I could become a star. I didn't want to be the person who got to the top and forgot about everyone. I tried to bring everyone with me. I tried to shine my light on those who I felt lacked recognition and exposure. I never wanted to be the only one who made it out. That was my setback, and I forgive myself. Like I always say, *God seen everything. He knows my heart and He knows my intentions were pure from day one.* I never hung around anyone to benefit from them. I was there during the darkest times. I believed in my friends more than I believed in myself. It wasn't because they had more talent, it was because I felt they lacked motivation. I knew I could do it without them, but I never wanted that to be the way my story was written. I will no longer chase after people who constantly show me that they can live without me. I have bigger challenges at hand. I have to dedicate my time and energy to the plans God has for me. What's for me will be for me and those who are supposed to be in my life will remain. *I forgive all but never forget nothing.*

# 16
# Millionaire Mindset

<u>2025</u>

I am thankful I had a chance to share my story, up until this point of my life, with the world. Once again, this book wasn't written to intentionally put anyone *in their feelings* or create enemies. I wanted to tell my life story so everyone could get a better understanding of who I am and what I've been through. I didn't want anyone to try to tell my story for me because nobody knows me like I know myself.

I want this book to encourage people to never give up. No matter how many times people tell you that you are not worthy, don't quit. No matter how many obstacles you encounter along the way, don't quit. The closest people to you sometimes will be the same people you have to stray away from and continue your mission without. Do not let your love for people who don't reciprocate the same love be your downfall. If they do not see your vision, how you see it, don't waste your time trying to prove anything to them.

Now that I have all of *that* out of my system, I would love to put my past behind me. I would love to focus on my future endeavors. By the time this book is released I will be 35 years old. It is true, us 90s babies are becoming real adults. I am thankful

I don't look *nothing* like what I've been through. Every time I tell someone my age, they never believe me. They assume I'm 10 years younger. I always tell people God blessed me with the fountain of youth. He knew I spent a lot of my years in my career trying to help others, so He didn't allow me to age. I still can go into the gym and lift the same amount of weight I lifted in high school; in fact, I am even stronger. I still have that creative imagination I had as a child that allows me to be innovative in today's time.

I'm at the age in life where I'm old enough to reach the generation above me and I still can relate to the new generation. I have a lot of young adults who study my moves daily. They read all my posts and are very interested in my life. I try to be more of a big brother to them instead of a father. I let them see the uncut version of my journey. I let them see that I am not perfect, and I also make mistakes just like them. I want to be able to display my life's obstacles to them, so they know how to maneuver through them quicker than me.

I would like to take the time out to say, *long live De'Vyon Collins.* De'Vyon is my younger cousin who was murdered in 2020 at the age of 19. He died a few days after I chose to move away and start a new life in Atlanta. My little cousin was one of the young adults who studied my life. He saw me in the *streets* making fast money, carrying guns, and hanging with criminals. He thought he could duplicate that lifestyle, however his life was taken from him at such a young age. Two weeks before he was murdered, I told him the *street life* isn't the life he wants to live. I did it because I felt it was something I *had* to do. No one believed in me, and I didn't know any other way. I told him I believed in him, and I wish he was still here with us. I love you, little cousin.

Summer 2025 will make the 20th year since the first day I hopped off the porch in 2005. I am thankful for everything I have been through and for the people who played a role in my life. Whether it was a good experience or bad experience, it made me the man I am today.

This book was released with a studio album, both titled, "I Was Slept On". Correct me if I am wrong, I am the first independent artist in the history of hip-hop to release an album and book at the same time on the same day. I have no plans of becoming a famous rap artist. I just want to finally give it everything I got and put myself first for the first time in my career. The album consists of all the hit singles from my first three mastered mixtapes. It will consist of singles from my tape, "Money & Musik" which I released when I was 18 years old and hit singles from my tape, "10 Years Later" which I released at 25 years old. And it will include hit singles from my tape, "Realer Than

Most" which I released at 29 years old. I also have a few additions to, "I Was Slept On" that were recorded and released as hit singles.

I put this project together because I want the world to catch up to who I was before they get to see where I am going. I have been making great music and once you hear this album you will know for yourself. Now that I have a lot of experience in the music business, I know how to get my music heard. I know how to put myself in front of my target audience. God blessed me to be financially stable enough to do it all independently. Shout out to the few people on my team who have helped me make this possible.

Currently, "I Was Slept On," is the biggest project of my career and I will get the recognition I deserve. This project is everywhere, using the same formula I used as a teenager - posters hung, flyers in all the convenience stores, and college promo tours to tap into that market. I use social media to my advantage - the biggest platforms shout out my project and let their followers know I made history by being the first independent rapper to release a book and album at the same time. I conducted a lot of interviews on some of the biggest podcasts. My goal to make myself relevant and ensure the world hears my story, is becoming my reality.

I have a lot of unreleased music ready to be released that I recorded myself in my own studio. I used to dream of owning a studio and recording myself. I know my book and my music are relatable to a lot of people worldwide. I don't make trendy music; I make music based on how I'm feeling that day and what I've been through. I honestly believe this is what hip-hop has been missing. The authentic heart-felt music is at an all-time low and it is the perfect time for me to come in and give it the spark it has been missing.

Life outside of music - I have a lot of business ventures I am working on. I plan to open up a few barbershops and hire some barbers. I plan to open up a recording studio for the public and help guide up-and-coming artists. I plan on getting a mobile food truck to run our Superior Soul Supplements out of and sell the best smoothies you ever tasted. I also want to open up an apparel and shoe store to sell my *Realer Than Most* apparel and other independent clothing companies can sell their lines also. I will have the latest shoes released and some exclusive retro styles.

I recently graduated technical school and became a certified HVAC Technician. It was something my grandmother Joan always wanted me to do. She told me, "Please don't put all your eggs in one basket. Learn some trades to secure finances then chase your dreams." I plan on getting in the HVAC field and learning the ins and outs so

I can eventually start up my own business fixing customers' air conditioners and refrigerator units.

I also want to learn how to invest my profits into stocks, crypto, and real estate. I want to learn how to *day trade* to have my money make more money for me. I will eventually get into buying land and flipping properties. I am monetized on a lot of social media platforms, and I want to start vlogging my life more. I want to get more subscribers on my YouTube channel and start generating more money.

I am a man of many skills and eventually all of this will come to life for me. I am taking it day by day and I am trusting God's process. I just told you guys some of my plans that I haven't told anybody about. Every time I've told people my dreams, they've shot them down and tried to force me into believing they were impossible. I stopped being so open to others and started talking more to God. We drew up all these plans together. Everything you guys have seen me accomplish, God and I planned out together *beforehand.*

I am thankful to be in the position I am in. I am free. I am healthy. I am able. I will no longer put others before me. I have a family who needs me to succeed. I will be the one to break the generational curse and become my family's first-generation millionaire. I will help change the lives of many people worldwide. I pray my story reaches millions of people and motivates them to continue chasing their dreams. Like a friend of mine used to always tell me, "The only person who can stop you, is you." Let go of all the excuses, let go of all the grudges, and just move forward. Take some baby steps ahead and one day you will look back and say, "Wow, I came a long way!"

If I can do it, so can you. I was slept on!

**-The End-**

**To be continued . . .**

Stay in touch:

www.trayplus321.com

Follow Tray Plus on all platforms:

@trayplus321